2 to 22 DAYS IN CALIFORNIA

THE ITINERARY PLANNER

ROGER RAPOPORT

John Muir Publications
Santa Fe, New Mexico

For Elizabeth, who knows the way.

Other books by Roger Rapoport
Is the Library Burning (with Laurence J. Kirshbaum)
The Great American Bomb Machine
The Superdoctors
The California Catalogue (with Margot Lind)
The Big Player (with Kenneth S. Uston)
California Dreaming: The Political Odyssey of Pat and Jerry Brown
Great Cities of Eastern Europe
Into the Sunlight: Life After the Iron Curtain
2 to 22 Days in Asia (with Burl Willes)
2 to 22 Days in the Rockies
22 Days Around the World (with Burl Willes)

John Muir Publications, P.O. Box 613, Santa Fe, NM 87504
© 1988, 1990, 1992, 1993, 1994, 1995 by Roger Rapoport
Cover and maps © 1988, 1990, 1992, 1993, 1994, 1995 by John Muir Publications

ISSN 1068-3003
ISBN 1-56261-203-4

Distributed to the book trade by
Publishers Group West
Emeryville, California

Design Mary Shapiro
Maps Holly Wood
Cover Photo Leo de Wys Inc./E. C. Stangler
Typography Sarah Johansson/Go West Graphics
Printer Banta Company

CONTENTS

ACKNOWLEDGMENTS

Portions of this book have appeared in different form in several publications. Thanks to my agent Philippa Brophy at the Sterling Lord Agency, Burl Willes, Rick Steves, Jo Ellen Teele, Ro Peterson, Mallory Smith, Karla Peterson, John Epstein, Tamara La Chimia, John Blades, Michael Forbes, Kristine Fister, and Claire Neubert.

My children, Jonathan and Elizabeth, eternal scouts in the quest for the perfect three-star sightseeing highlight, were a constant source of aid and comfort. Also thanks to Lisa Cohn for her work on this updated edition.

Please Note
Although the author has made every effort to ensure accuracy, readers are advised to inquire locally, particularly regarding museum/attraction hours and routings, which are subject to change. We suggest readers supplement this book with current local maps. Prices mentioned in the book are approximate and subject to change. Because the least expensive rooms tend to be booked first, you may be asked to pay more than the minimum rates quoted. A number of the roads that form part of the 22-day itinerary are mountainous and in a few cases not suitable for oversize or recreational vehicles. You should carry chains in the mountains during the winter months and be prepared for sudden storms that can block access during other times of the year. Check the weather forecast before setting out for the Sierra region. Comments or suggestions written to the author in care of the publisher are welcome.

HOW TO USE THIS BOOK

This book, which begins at a zoo in San Diego and ends three weeks later in an Oakland ice cream parlor, covers the length and breadth of California. Along the way you'll stand on the point where Juan Rodriguez Cabrillo discovered this region for Spain, see the back lot that was the setting for Bogie and Bacall in *Casablanca*, and explore William Randolph Hearst's cathedral to capitalism. This trip will give you a chance to walk the land John Steinbeck and John Muir called home, visit Jack London's palace for pigs, and see the grave of California's man with a mission, Father Junípero Serra.

This itinerary gives you a chance to hike amid some of the tallest and biggest trees in the world. You'll visit beaches that have inspired movie legends and see parks that are home to wildlife seldom seen outside of California. Along the shore you may discover gleaming pieces of jade and agate, or scoop up brightly colored glass worn smooth by the surf. In the foothills you'll see remnants of the greatest treasure hunt the West has ever known and have a chance to pan for gold. Up in the mountains there will be time to picnic at the top of a waterfall that often runs under a rainbow's arch.

While nature gets star billing, the state's notable man-made attractions figure prominently in this rewarding journey. At one amusement park you'll enjoy an electrical parade and fireworks that turn every summer night into the Fourth of July. There'll be an opportunity to visit what are possibly the handsomest Victorian hotels in America and certainly the nation's best-known prison. You'll find convenient accommodations and campgrounds in all price ranges as well as ideal settings for golf, tennis, surfing, and biking. Also suggested are restaurants popular for their food, culinary tradition, and in several cases, their commanding views. Whether you seek haute cuisine or hot dogs, there'll always be a promising choice close at hand.

This book comes—in the parlance of auto dealers— fully loaded. Numerous itinerary options and extensions give you the opportunity to augment the basic 22-day itinerary as your time and interests allow. As you begin planning your trip, feel free to adjust this 22-day schedule to meet your needs. (More on that subject later.) But first let's take a look at the itinerary format. It is divided into 22 daily sections, each containing:

1. A **suggested schedule** for each day's travel and sightseeing.

2. A detailed **travel route** description for each driving segment of your trip.

3. Descriptive **overviews** and **sightseeing highlights** (rated in order of importance for the day in question: ▲▲▲ Don't miss; ▲▲ Try hard to see; and ▲ See if you get a chance).

4. Suggested **restaurants** and **lodging** or **campgrounds** for each night of the trip.

5. **Helpful hints**—random tidbits that will help make your trip go well.

6. **Itinerary options**—excursion suggestions for travelers who have more time.

7. User-friendly **maps** designed to show you what the road up ahead is really like.

Why Take the 22-Day Approach?

If you're new to the 2 to 22 Days itinerary planner concept, perhaps you have some questions about this approach to travel planning. Most travelers visiting a new area rely on the advice of travel agents, tourism offices, auto clubs, and guidebooks to plan a successful trip. Others simply put themselves in the hands of a reliable tour operator and hope for the best. As a travel writer who has lived and written in California for the past 20 years, I spend a lot of time debriefing people who visit and love all the areas you are about to see. Planning a trip can be a challenge. Blending the various interests of your party, scheduling around museums that operate on varying schedules, finding the most scenic route, and finding a centrally located hotel are some of the issues crucial to any traveler. That's why I'm so enthusiastic about the 2 to 22 Days approach. Created by Rick Steves, a Seattle travel writer and tour leader, the first guide was based on the itinerary he taught in classes for prospective European visitors. Rick frequently had plane tickets, Eurail passes, even cash lying around the office. No one ever touched those valuables. But one thing did frequently disappear from the office: his 2 to 22 Days itinerary. Tired of making repeated trips to the copying machine, he turned his master travel plan over to John Muir Publications. The success of his European itinerary planners has led to similar guides covering other destinations around the world, including California.

This book—in effect, the trip of my dreams—proves that travel writers have no secrets. All the personal favorites I share with my best friends are yours to enjoy. One of the pleasures of working on this volume was an opportunity to revisit each of these regions to design the best itinerary. I invite you to discover the best of California and to tell your friends about your discoveries. In this way, we are rewarding people who, through considerable effort in our behalf, make California a favorite destination of world travelers.

As you make your way through the state, bear in mind that the 2 to 22 Days plan is not necessarily one you have to enjoy in a single trip. If your time is limited, say, to only a week, consider following the first-, second-, or third-week itinerary to see either southern, central, or northern California. If you are on a business trip to Los Angeles and have only a free weekend, by all means focus on that portion of the book and save the rest for a return visit. Because most of the major destinations in this book have good air service, you can easily jump between regions to sample different parts of the state. Feel free to adjust or augment the suggested itineraries as you see fit.

If you've already signed up for a tour, or are traveling with a group, you may not be sure about how to use this book. Consider the wisdom of one of our finest travel writers, Paul Theroux, who suggests the best strategy in a distant land is to "travel with a group and, when it suits you, drop out." Every tour allows for a considerable amount of free time, even free days. Some give you several free pre- or posttour days. Use these opportunities to pursue some of the suggestions in this book. Like a local guide—who might charge $100 a day or more—this book helps you discover areas many tourists miss. Or, if you prefer, break off from long lunches, shopping tours, or other less-than-critical events of organized "tourdom," to follow a few of my suggestions. It's not even unknown for experienced travelers to leave a tour for a day or two to pursue an itinerary of their own making.

If you're not sure about breaking away and taking advantage of some of the book's promising suggestions, permit me to digress for a moment. On a recent tour of the Great Wall, near Beijing, I decided to take leave of my group. My motivation was simple: the wall tour was cut short to permit the group to enjoy a two-hour banquet and a shopping trip at a somewhat overpriced "Friendship" store. By going on my own, I was the only member of our group who actually had time to climb to the top of the wall. While everyone else was scrambling down to oblige the whistle-blowing tour leader, I was able to relax, shoot pictures, and enjoy this memorable experience. Back at the entrance I noticed a big sign touting the terra-cotta warriors on display 1,000 miles away at Xian. It seemed odd to me that this—probably the most important Chinese archaeological find of the century, one that was being sold at our group's hotel as a three-day, $300, side trip—was promoted here. Then it hit me: perhaps there was a traveling exhibit. It took me about five minutes to find someone to translate the sign. I couldn't believe my luck! Just a couple of minutes down the road a small museum was exhibiting a third of the terra-cotta warriors. I ran to the exhibit, paid the equivalent of 15 cents for admission, and enjoyed this fantastic display in the company of many Chinese tourists. I was the only Caucasian in the museum. Later, I mentioned my good fortune to members of the tour who were on what they characterized as a once-in-a-lifetime tour of China. They were mortified at the thought of having been led away from a world-famous treasure to shop for silk. Later, when I talked to one of the Chinese guides about it, he brushed the issue aside: "The terra-cotta soldiers weren't that important."

While this itinerary is necessarily selective, rest assured that you will never be rushed past a landmark because the owner of a restaurant or store has greased your local guide's palm with silver. My intent is to help you find the treasures that distinguish California from, say, Nebraska or Ohio. Although the book guides, it never dictates. It can even benefit the kind of person who believes vacations are meant to be spent poolside at a resort. This book gives you a chance to survey the landscape, find the spots that suit you best, and then settle in. If other members of your party don't like sitting around, hand them the book. They can follow the suggested itineraries—while you get to know all the towel boys on a first-name basis.

How Much Will It Cost?

To create a budget for this trip, begin by estimating your per diem expenses. Budget travelers can figure on spending about $50 to $70 a night on a hotel room for two. A moderate room will run an average of $70 to $100. If you're in a deluxe mode, figure $100 to $200 a night. Bed and breakfasts average about $60 to $125 per night, slightly less for home stays. Hostels average about $10 per night. You can camp in public parks for $10 to $30 a night, while private campgrounds run about $20 to $35 per night.

If you're driving in your own car, base gas estimates on approximately 1,700 miles within California, plus mileage from your home to San Diego and back from San Francisco. If you are flying or taking the train to California, expect to pay about $175 to $250 per week for a compact rental car, plus drop charges. You may be able to do better if you go with a subcompact and return the car to the renting location.

To calculate food costs, figure inexpensive restaurant costs at under $15 for dinner, moderate establishments at $15 to $40, and expensive choices at over $40.

Budget about $7 per person per meal for breakfast and lunch. If you are doing your own cooking or picnicking for lunch (as I do), these meals will cost about the same as they do at home.

Admission to state and national parks averages $4 to $8. Most of the museums on our tour are under $5, and many are free. A day at Disneyland will run about $75 to $100 per person (including meals). Figure a total of $125 per person for other recommended tours such as Moaning Cavern, the Columbia Gold Mine Tour, and Alcatraz. Naturally, you'll want to add in the price of any special interest tours, bike rentals, or horseback tours.

When to Go
Because California is a year-round destination, you can plan this trip for any season. With the exception of Days 10, 11, and 12 in Yosemite, you're not likely to encounter any snow. Count on moderate weather year-round. Spring and fall—excellent times to avoid crowds—usually have less fog than summer. Many visitors enjoy coming in September and October, California's Indian summer season. In September, beaches are still warm enough for swimming, and toward the end of the month you can enjoy fall colors in the mountains. If you are interested in rafting, come in late spring when rivers are highest.

Summertime, of course, is peak season. Although it can get hot, particularly in the south and redwood country, there's always a nearby stream where you can cool off. My preference is for an early summer visit because the crowds are smaller, the waterfalls are better, and the streams run higher. Although the north coast can be wet in winter, some of the best weather I've ever seen here was in the middle of December. Winter, by the way, is also a fine time to visit Yosemite: although access is restricted on some of the trails and many campgrounds are closed, you can enjoy the ice rink, ski at Badger Pass, and take a cross-country trip through the Big Trees Grove.

Culturally speaking, the Christmas season is an excellent time to visit California, particularly the big cities where many hotels offer special discount rates. Numerous festivals and special events are offered during this time of year and the weather remains mild. Whenever you come, be sure to pack some warm clothes for the mountains and those windy San Francisco days.

Remember to double-check for holiday closings. Many museums and attractions are closed on Thanksgiving, Christmas, New Year's Day, and other holidays.

Transportation

Amtrak's Coast Starlight parallels the recommended driving route from San Diego to San Luis Obispo, where there's a bus connection to San Simeon. The train takes the inland route to Salinas, where there is a connection to Monterey, and then continues north to San Francisco. Make your reservations as far in advance as possible. There's also a rail/bus connection to Yosemite Valley on the unreserved San Joaquin. Bus and air service is available to all the major points covered in this itinerary. Nonetheless, my preference is a car or RV trip. Although there are a few stretches of unpaved road, you won't need a 4-wheel-drive vehicle. Very large RVs will not be able to navigate some of the rural trips such as Davidson Road in Humboldt County. The only conditional route on this itinerary is Highway 152 over Pacheco Pass: please read and heed the advice about this road in Day 10. Keep in mind that vehicle rental insurance is invalid when you are driving on unpaved roads. To check on road conditions in northern California, call Caltrans at (510) 654-9890. In southern California, call (213) 626-7231. Exercise extreme caution driving at night in mountain areas, especially in the winter months.

Before leaving home, you'll want to check out your vehicle to make sure that it can handle steep mountain grades, hot- and cold-weather driving, and back roads. Although you'll never be more than about 25 miles from emergency road service, you can avoid frustration by carrying a basic auto tool kit and repair manual, spare V-belts, radiator hoses, a good spare tire, and extra radiator coolant.

Should you plan on renting an RV in California, consider choosing a mini motor home: you'll appreciate their maneuverability and relatively decent gas mileage; large motor homes are recommended only for groups of more than four. I'd suggest picking your RV up on Day 5 in the Los Angeles area. You'll find it cheaper to start out by renting a car in San Diego and dropping it in Los Angeles. That way you won't be burdened with a large vehicle while visiting those two metropolitan areas. A number of national chains, such as U-Haul, Budget, and Cruise America rent RVs in the Los Angeles area. The Los Angeles Convention and Visitors Bureau at 515 South Figueroa, Los Angeles 90071, (213) 624-7300, can suggest additional RV rental companies.

Food and Lodging

Along the way I've suggested many restaurants in all price categories. In addition to well-known establishments, I've included a sampling of newer dining spots serving popular regional and ethnic cuisine: you'll have a chance to enjoy specialties like petrale sole, pastrami on rye, fajitas, calzone, and fresh oysters. Good hot dogs and giant ice-cream sundaes are also on the menu. Since man or woman does not live by food alone, the itinerary also includes fine dining spots with views you won't soon forget. Naturally, I also suggest picnic spots for lunch: this is not only a good way to save money but a pleasant way to visit some of the state's fine parks. A lightweight cooler stocked from a local deli is a must for any serious California traveler.

If you're planning to stay in hotels, you'll find it's easier to get reservations in rural areas during the week. I'd recommend reservations if you plan to visit Santa Barbara, Carmel, or La Jolla on a weekend, in peak season, or during a holiday period. With the exception of midweek during the winter, reservations are always a good idea at Yosemite. In general, availability in the cities is much better on weekends and holidays, when many hotels offer discounts. If you have your heart set on a particular big city hotel during the week, a reservation may be a good idea, especially if you want the best room rate.

Because many B&Bs have a limited number of rooms, it's not a bad idea to book ahead, particularly on weekends and during holiday seasons; don't overlook the B&B reservation services if you're having trouble finding a place at the last minute.

For youth hostel information, contact Golden Gate Council, 425 Divisadero Street, Suite 306, San Francisco, CA 94117; (415) 863-9939. Naturally, all prices listed are approximate and subject to change. If you book any accommodation using a credit card, ask the reservationist not to put the charge through until you actually show up. Unfortunately, credit card companies put a hold against your account for each reservation; that hold is often not lifted until a week or more after you've checked out. This process can eat up your available credit. Tell the reservationist to simply keep your card number on file against the remote possibility that you won't show up; that way large holds won't mount up on your card. Incidentally, toll-free 800 numbers are a good way to save money. Since they change frequently, don't despair if your call doesn't go through on the first try. Double-check by calling directory assistance at (800) 555-1212.

State and national park campground reservations can be dear. Book ahead, particularly during peak season. Call (800) 444-7275, or write to Mistix, P.O. Box 85705, San Diego, CA 92138-5705. This company also handles San Simeon reservations.

Alternatively, look for less congested national forest, county, or private campgrounds. The state park system does offer some overflow camping space in popular areas like the Humboldt County redwood parks. One final suggestion: two popular stops on our trip, San Simeon and Alcatraz, both take advance reservations. Book ahead for these landmarks. Consult Days 7 and 16 for specific details.

Recommended Reading
Carey McWilliams's *California the Great Exception* is an excellent introduction to the state's political and social history. Kevin Starr's books, *Americans and the*

California Dream 1850-1915 and *Inventing the Dream: California Through the Progressive Era*, are also highly recommended. *The World Rushed In*, by J. S. Holliday, provides a good overview of the gold rush. *A Companion to California*, by James D. Hart, is a fine reference book that will quickly answer many questions about the state's leading citizens, communities, and landmarks.

Among the many general and regional travel books, the one likely to be the most useful to you on this 22-day trip is the *California Coastal Resource Guide*. Another book that's fun to read is *The California Highway 1 Book*. You may want to pick up one of the general guidebooks to the state such as *Birnbaum's*. If you have an interest in B&Bs, I recommend *The Complete Guide to Bed & Breakfasts, Inns & Guesthouses* by Pamela Lanier; it includes numerous suggestions across California and also lists many B&B reservation services.

For current suggestions on restaurants, shows, and galleries, check the local dailies such as the *Los Angeles Times*, *San Francisco Chronicle*, or *Oakland Tribune*. *Los Angeles*, *San Diego* and *Focus* magazines also provide helpful tips for visitors.

Special Note

Have a good time in the water, but don't underestimate the power of the ocean, particularly in California. Never turn your back to the ocean or swim alone. If you are caught in a riptide, swim parallel to the shore to avoid wearing yourself out until it's safe to return to the beach. All California coastal waters are under 75 degrees, which means you are losing body heat while you're swimming in the ocean. Take periodic breaks to warm up. It's not uncommon for waves to suddenly sweep up on coastal bluffs: keep an eye out for them. Children must remain under adult supervision *at all times* when you are near the beach.

Where to Start

2 to 22 Days in California is essentially a border-to-border coastal trip with a cross-state visit to Yosemite and the Gold Country. I recommend starting in San Diego, where Cabrillo discovered what is now California. It's easily reached by air, train, or freeway. If you're coming from another direction, feel free to alter the itinerary as you see fit.

For readers with less time, here are some ways to adapt the trip plan:

■ Southern California: Days 1-7 cover San Diego, Disneyland, Los Angeles, Santa Barbara, and San Simeon.

■ Central California: Days 7-14 cover San Simeon, Big Sur, Carmel, Monterey, Yosemite, the Gold Country, and ends in San Francisco.

■ Northern California: Days 14-22 cover the Bay Area, North Coast, Redwood Country, and Sonoma Valley.

Here are suggestions for short trips:

■ San Diego and Disneyland: Days 1-3.
■ Disneyland and Los Angeles: Days 3-5.
■ Los Angeles and Santa Barbara: Days 4-6.
■ Santa Barbara, San Simeon, and Carmel: Days 7-9.
■ Yosemite and the Gold Country: Days 10-13.
■ The Bay Area: Days 14-16 and 22.
■ North Coast and Redwood Country: Days 17-20.
■ Sonoma Valley: Days 20 and 21.

22 Days in California

DAY 1 Arrive in San Diego. Visit the zoo and see the Chinese pandas, the penguin exhibit, and the unsurpassed hummingbird enclosure. Explore Balboa Park and the Aerospace Historical Center. Dinner in Old Town.

DAY 2 Your day begins with a visit to Sea World. From here, proceed to Coronado Island for lunch at the Hotel Del Coronado, one of the West's best-loved Victorian hotels. In the afternoon, head north to the Scripps Aquarium and hit one of the popular beaches. Eat dinner

2 to 22 Days in California

and stroll on Prospect Street in La Jolla, then have a nightcap at La Valencia Hotel overlooking the Pacific.

DAY 3 Disneyland without tears: how to get the most out of the West's leading vacation destination.

DAY 4 On the ultimate Hollywood backstage tour at the Warner Studios, you may see television or feature films being shot. Alternatively, take a trip to razzle-dazzle Universal Studios for an entertaining overview of motion picture making. In the afternoon, art buffs will head for the Huntington Museum in San Marino while students of history will explore the Southwest Museum and the home of its founder, pioneer journalist Charles Lummis. Dinner at The Pantry in downtown Los Angeles, Musso and Frank in Hollywood, or Canter's on Fairfax.

Optional Extension: Catalina

DAY 5 Your day begins in the Late Cretaceous period at the La Brea Tar Pits and moves on to Beverly Hills, Will Rogers State Park, and the Getty Museum.

Optional Extension: Malibu

Optional Extension: Ojai

DAY 6 Tour Santa Barbara: the museums, the splendid Spanish-Moorish courthouse, the historic adobes, the Arlington Theater, the superb Museum of Natural History, the beach, and Montecito.

DAY 7 Visit San Simeon, California's ultimate house designed by Julia Morgan and paid for by William Randolph Hearst.

DAY 8 Drive up the legendary Big Sur coast, with stops at Jade Cove, the waterfalls of Julia Pfeiffer-Burns State Park, and the Henry Miller Library. After a visit to Pfeiffer Beach, continue to Point Lobos and Carmel/Monterey.

DAY 9 Visit the Carmel Mission, Carmel-By-The-Sea, the 17 Mile Drive, Monterey Bay Aquarium, Cannery Row, and historic Monterey.

DAY 10 Enjoy a morning stop at the loveliest of California's mission towns, San Juan Bautista, followed by a leisurely drive across the San Joaquin Valley to Yosemite National Park.

DAY 11 Breakfast at the Ahwahnee Hotel is followed by a relaxed bike ride to the visitor center, Happy Isles, Vernal Falls, and Mirror Lake.

DAY 12 Drive to the Mariposa Big Trees Grove, the Pioneer Yosemite History Center at Wawona, and Glacier Point. After visiting Sentinel Dome, return to Yosemite Valley.

Optional Extension: Mono Lake and Bodie

DAY 13 Drive through Big Oak Flat and historic Chinese Camp to the rail museum at Jamestown, and pan for gold in Columbia. Overnight at Columbia, the restored gold rush town.

Optional Extension: Northern Gold Country, Lake Tahoe, Sacramento

DAY 14 Walk or rappel your way down Moaning Cavern. Visit the locust-shaded gold rush village of Murphys, followed by a drive across the Sacramento River delta to the San Francisco Bay area. A cable car takes you to dinner on Fisherman's Wharf.

DAY 15 Walk the Filbert Steps to the top of Telegraph Hill and then explore the historic Maritime Museum. Drive through Pacific Heights, continue to Fort Point for a picnic. Cross the Golden Gate Bridge to visit the Marin Headlands and Sausalito before returning to San Francisco.

DAY 16 Your Alcatraz tour is followed by a visit to Golden Gate Park and lunch at Stow Lake. Drive back through Sea Cliff, the Clement Street neighborhood, and Pacific Heights to North Beach. Visit Chinatown and Union Square.

DAY 17 One of California's finest drives takes you through the pastoral Anderson Valley to Mendocino and Fort Bragg. Today you'll see one of California's best coastal parks, Russian Gulch, and the Mendocino Botanical Gardens.

DAY 18 A stop at Glass Beach in Fort Bragg is followed by a drive through the Avenue of the Giants to the Scotia Mill. After seeing the Victorian dairy town of Ferndale, continue to Eureka and the Carson Mansion.

DAY 19 After breakfast at the Samoa Cookhouse, stop at the Clarke Museum and then continue on to Redwood National Park. After lunch, visit the Roosevelt Elk Preserve, Fern Canyon, and Lost Man Creek. Dinner on the coast at Trinidad.

DAY 20 Return south through redwood country to Jack London State Historic Park and the Sonoma Valley.

DAY 21 The Sonoma walking tour includes the Mission, Vallejo Home, Barracks, and a Gothic revival church. You'll also see California's oldest premium winery.

Optional Extension: Napa Valley

DAY 22 Tour the University of California at Berkeley campus, then lunch at Chez Panisse. In the afternoon visit the state's leading Californiana collection at the Oakland Museum. Dessert at a famous ice cream parlor.

SAN DIEGO

Like Juan Rodriguez Cabrillo, who claimed California for Spain in 1542, your visit to this region begins in San Diego. He loved it and so will you. Considered by many travelers to be America's most desirable vacation city, this border town is an excellent place to start your trip. People who say they don't like to vacation in cities have probably never been to San Diego. You'll find access by plane, train, or car a pleasure. The airport is only 3 miles from downtown and about 20 minutes from most major tourist destinations. The train station is equally convenient. Motorists will find the city an easy place to get around in.

About the only problem you may have with San Diego is deciding between all the enticing opportunities set out before you. Millions of people visit this popular resort city each year to take advantage of its fine beaches, world-class zoo, good shopping, and pleasing restaurants and nightlife. You can even enjoy a glimpse of Mexico. While there's plenty to keep you busy here, San Diego remains a relaxed vacation center. Most major attractions are within half an hour of one another. Dining in outdoor restaurants in Old Town, strolling La Jolla's posh Prospect Avenue, or simply exploring the museums of Balboa Park are among the city's many pleasures. Because it's sunny more than 300 days a year, you can plan on getting in some golf, jogging, cycling, or tennis nearly any time you visit.

As you might imagine, this relaxed environment makes San Diego a popular choice with retirees. You'll also notice a strong military presence here as this is the home of the Commander Naval Base San Diego. And while the city may seem low-key and laid-back, it is also an important center of medical, marine, electronic, and aerospace research. Several of the best-known scholarly centers, such as Scripps Institution and the Salk Institute, welcome visitors. The handsome University of California campus at La Jolla is also worth visiting. Although San

Diego is a city of the future, it has skillfully avoided
many of the planning mistakes made by other urban centers. The result is a community that has enhanced its natural bays, created vast parks in which you can entertain
yourself all day, and protected its architectural assets. In
short, California's birthplace is the ideal place to begin
your 22-day tour.

Suggested Schedule	
8:00 a.m.	Breakfast.
9:00 a.m.	San Diego Zoo.
2:00 p.m.	Museum of Man, or Reuben H. Fleet Space Theater.
4:00 p.m.	Old Town/Heritage Park.
7:00 p.m.	Nightlife.

Travel Route
Most of today's attractions are located along the Interstate
5 corridor in San Diego. If you arrive by plane at San
Diego International Airport, rent a car there. Follow
North Harbor Drive around the airport and jog left on
Laurel Street, which will put you on Interstate 5. If you
plan to rent an RV, wait until the end of your Los
Angeles visit on Day 5. Rail passengers will want to
arrange for rental car pickup at the downtown train station. If you're driving, you'll most likely arrive from the
north on Interstate 5 or from the east on Interstate 8.

For information on reaching your hotel, consult the
Lodging section. After checking in, you'll want to take
Interstate 5 north from downtown and exit east on Laurel
Street to Balboa Park and the San Diego Zoo.

Sightseeing Highlights
▲▲▲**San Diego Zoo**—One of the world's great zoos is
located in Balboa Park, just a few minutes from downtown. Take the Laurel Street exit off Interstate 5. The
1,074-acre park is the city's cultural hub and the zoo its
most popular attraction. Tiger River, Gorilla Tropics, and
Sun Bear Forest are three of the latest additions to the

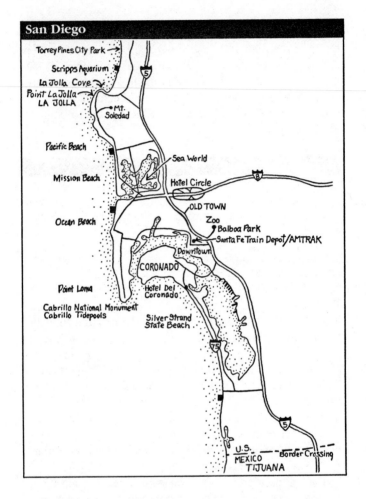

San Diego

100-acre tropical garden showcasing a 3,900-animal menagerie. The collection includes many rare and endangered species seldom seen in zoos, such as long-billed kiwis, wild Przewalski's horses, and golden marmosets. A guided 40-minute bus tour is the best way to get an overview of the zoo. Then wander about to enjoy a closer look.

A children's zoo scaled to size for a four-year-old gives kids a chance to pet baby animals and watch attendants bottle-feed and diaper young primates. From the orangutans to the Galápagos tortoises, this zoo is a place of endless fascination. This sanctuary also has probably the best outdoor penguin display in America. Be sure not to miss the hummingbird enclosure, where these iridescent birds dart around you. It's about as close to heaven as most of us are likely to get in this world.

▲▲**Balboa Park Museums**—Just south of the zoo is El Prado, the promenade that serves as the hub for seven major museums found in Balboa Park. The Natural History Museum has a good exhibit on shore ecology, and the Aerospace Historical Center, located in the Palisades Area, covers air travel from the biplane to early space exploration. The Museum of Photographic Arts, Hall of Champions Sports Museum, and San Diego Museum of Art are also excellent. Be sure to see the Museum of Man, dedicated to our physical and cultural past. They are open daily from 10:00 a.m. to 4:30 p.m., except for the Museum of Art, which is closed Mondays. The Reuben H. Fleet Space Theater and Science Center has a major planetarium, touchable exhibits that will delight children, and changing Omnimax films. Call (619) 238-1168 for times and feature titles. Open daily 9:45 a.m. to 9:30 p.m. For just $9.50 you can purchase a passport at any of these museums. This passport contains coupons which can be used in different combinations for admission to 2 to 4 musuems.

Old Town—When you leave the park, return to Interstate 5 and head north to the Old Town exit. This is the place to find old newspaper offices, restored adobes, stables, museums, and the ancestral home of Leo Carillo, who played Pancho in *The Cisco Kid* An important part of any visit here is shopping at Bazar Del Mundo, a good place to find Mexican handicrafts and other quality imports. The plaza's patio restaurants are a good choice for a drink. While in the Old Town area you'll want to visit Heritage Park, a group of landmark buildings that includes the city's first synagogue—Temple Beth Israel—and the Sherman-Gilbert House. During World War II the navy instructed the owners of this Eastlake stick-style residence, the Gilbert sisters, to install a light on the third-story tower to prevent plane crashes. Being true Victorians, they avoided adding that sign of impropriety by simply removing the tower. Fortunately, they saved all the pieces, which have been reassembled for the enjoyment of future generations.

Nightlife

After dining in Old Town you may want to return to your hotel and call it a day. But why not wind up your first day in California by sampling some of the city's nightlife, jazz, or theater? Perhaps best known is Balboa Park's **Old Globe Theater**, where you can enjoy Shakespeare in repertory with other classic and contemporary plays during the summer months. Call (619) 239-2255. Other popular little theaters include the **La Jolla Playhouse**, (619) 534-3960, and the **San Diego Repertory Theater**, a lyceum theater in the colorful Horton Plaza downtown, (619) 235-8025. Jazz fans may want to try **Croce's**, a restaurant/club owned by the widow of the late singer/composer, Jim Croce. Against a backdrop of artifacts commemorating the star who died in a plane crash, you'll hear live bebop, blues, and fusion. It's located downtown at 802 Fifth Avenue, (619) 233-4355. If you prefer jazz, contemporary or '60s sounds, why not try the **Cannibal Bar** at the Catamaran Hotel, 3999 Mission Boulevard in Mission Beach north of downtown, (619) 488-1081; open Wednesday through Saturday. A well-established restaurant/disco is the often-packed **Diego's** at 860 Garnett in Pacific Beach, (619) 272-1241. For a good laugh try the **Improv** at 832 Garnet Avenue, (619) 483-4520, or the **Comedy Store** at 916 Pearl Street, La Jolla, (619) 454-9176.

Lodging

Hotel Circle: Located off Interstate 8, east of Interstate 5, this area is ten minutes north of downtown and has the largest concentration of San Diego lodging. There are also numerous establishments near the airport on Shelter Island and in the downtown area. If you're looking for a moderately priced establishment on Hotel Circle, consider **Town and Country Hotel** at 500 Hotel Circle North, San Diego 92108, (800) 854-2608 nationwide or (800) 542-6082 in

California. This high-rise offers some quad rooms year-round beginning at about $95, a good value in that you have a choice of four swimming pools and are close to the zoo and to Sea World. Near the airport and Sea World, **Loma Lodge** at 3202 Rosecrans is a good budget choice. Ask for a room on the back, under $40; (619) 222-0511.

B&Bs: The **Keating House Inn,** a grand, late-19th-century Queen Anne, is convenient to all the attractions at Balboa Park, as well as to downtown and the Mission Bay Area. It's located at 2331 Second Avenue, San Diego, 92101. Rooms run $50 to $110. (619) 239-8585. Other B&Bs can be booked around the city through two referral services: **Bed and Breakfast Directory for San Diego**, P.O. Box 3292, San Diego, CA 92163, telephone (619) 297-3130, can refer you to B&B units ranging in price from $50 to $250; **Boat and Breakfast—San Diego** at 1450 Harbor Island Drive, San Diego, CA 92101, offers nightly yacht rentals from $90 to $250.

La Jolla: Hotels here are about 20 minutes north of downtown and worth the extra drive; this is my favorite place to stay in San Diego. To reach this area, exit Interstate 5 west at La Jolla Village Drive. Continue to Torrey Pines Road and make a left. Follow Torrey Pines to Prospect Street, where you turn right. Make another right on Coast Boulevard to reach the **La Jolla Cove Motel**, 1155 Coast Boulevard, San Diego 92037. This establishment has plain units, but one of the handsomest settings in southern California, on Scripps Park. Just step out onto your porch and you'll get a panoramic view of snorkelers, divers, surfers, and other California marine life. About $60 to $150 for rooms, studios, or suites. Call (800) 248-COVE or (619) 459-2621 and book early. **La Jolla Beach & Tennis Club**, 2000 Spindrift Drive, 92037, offers rooms beginning at $95. It offers a private beach, tennis, and golf. Call (619) 454-7126.

If you prefer a historic mission-style resort overlooking the Pacific, consider **La Valencia Hotel**, 1132 Prospect Street, San Diego 92037. This hotel has long been a popular hideaway for the rich and/or famous. Rooms are in the $150 to $295 range; (619) 454-0771 or (800) 451-0772. For the atrium life, try **Embassy Suites Hotel La Jolla** at 4550 La Jolla Village Drive (east of Interstate 5), San Diego 92122. This hotel is popular with families who enjoy the convenience of two rooms, complimentary breakfasts, and cocktails. It is about a ten-minute drive inland from the beach. Approximately $129 to $169. (800) EMBASSY or (619) 453-0400.

Coronado: South of downtown, reached via the Coronado Bridge, this community is best known for the **Hotel Del Coronado**, 1500 Orange Avenue, Coronado 92118. This century-old Victorian hotel is a national historic landmark and a very popular resort. Tennis courts, an Olympic-size pool, boat rentals, and a health spa are at your disposal. Rooms run $154 to $399. (619) 522-8000. Across the street from the Hotel Del Coronado is the **Glorietta Bay Inn**, 1630 Glorietta Boulevard, Coronado 92118. This historic Spreckels mansion has been converted into a lovely hotel close to the beach and shops. You can rent a bike here and explore Coronado Island. About $95 to $150. (619) 435-3101. In California call (800) 283-9383. Outside California call (800) 854-3380. **Le Meridien San Diego** at Coronado overlooking San Diego Bay has a spa and an extensive recreation program. Rooms cost $165 to $225, suites run $375 to $625; call (619) 435-3000 or (800) 543-4300.

Campers: If you enjoy water sports, why not stay on Mission Bay? **Campland on the Bay**, 2211 Pacific Beach Drive, San Diego 92109, comes with a marina, café, and grocery store. Rates run about $18.50 to $50. (619) 581-4200. Another possibility on the bay is **De Anza Harbor Resort**, 2727 De Anza Road, San Diego 92119. Spaces run about $20 to $33 and you can use the boat ramps. (619) 273-3214. **KOA San Diego Metro**, located 8 miles south of town at 111 North Second Avenue, Chula Vista, offers spaces for $23 to $32. (619) 427-3601. There are no public campgrounds in the immediate San Diego area.

Budget: The 50-bed **Point Loma Hostel** at 3790 Udall Street, San Diego 92107, is convenient to Sea World and Old Town. Open 8:00 a.m. to 10:00 a.m. and 5:30 p.m. to 10:00 p.m. daily. Bring your own bedding. Rates are $12 to $15. (619) 223-4778.

Food

Dobson's Bar and Restaurant, 956 Broadway Circle downtown, is a popular bistro offering country-style French cooking. The bar is nearly always jammed, (619) 231-6771. For good inexpensive food, try **El Indio Tortilla Shop**, 3695 Indio Street, San Diego (closed Sunday), (619) 299-0333. In Old Town try the **Old Town Mexican Café**, 2489 San Diego Avenue. A little loud but the carnitas are good. It is moderately priced and open until 11:00 p.m., (619) 297-4330. Fresh seafood buffs might want to try the salmon or calamari at Old Town's **Cafe Pacifica**, 2414 San Diego Avenue, San Diego, (619) 291-6666. For drinks, try one of the attractive outdoor restaurants on the nearby Old Town Plaza.

If you want outstanding hot dogs and good chili, take the kids to **Sluggo's** at 6980 La Jolla Boulevard, La Jolla, (619) 459-5536. Another excellent choice is **El Crab Catcher**, 1298 Prospect Street, La Jolla. Try the oyster bar at this restaurant overlooking La Jolla Cove, (619) 454-9587. **George's At The Cove**, 1250 Prospect Place in La Jolla, offers fine fish, meat, and fowl in the expensive dining room and a moderately priced lounge. There is also patio dining upstairs. Great view. (619) 454-4244.

Helpful Hint

For more visitor information, contact the San Diego Convention and Visitors Bureau at 1200 Third Avenue, Suite 824, San Diego, CA 92101. Or call (619) 236-1212. You can also stop by the International Visitor Information Center at 11 Horton Plaza.

AROUND SAN DIEGO

Today you'll have a chance to see some of the region's famed marine life parks and museums, best-known architectural landmarks, historic monuments, swank shopping districts, and, of course, memorable beaches. This is a day to work on your tan a little and try some more of the community's outdoor restaurants and sidewalk cafés. You'll also have a glimpse of California's affluent society in La Jolla. The pace is leisurely, allowing you time to sightsee, swim, shop, and explore some of the region's most attractive neighborhoods.

Suggested Schedule

8:00 a.m.	Breakfast at your hotel.
9:00 a.m.	Sea World.
1:00 p.m.	Lunch on Coronado Island or continue your visit to Sea World.
2:30 p.m.	Visit Point Loma or remain at Sea World.
3:30 p.m.	Stephen Birch Aquarium-Museum or beach-comb in La Jolla.
6:00 p.m.	Stroll Prospect Avenue in La Jolla.
6:30 p.m.	Dinner in La Jolla.
8:00 p.m.	Drive to Mount Soledad.

Sightseeing Highlights

▲▲**Sea World**—After breakfast, visit Sea World, a 150-acre marine life entertainment park at 1720 South Shores Road on Mission Bay (take Sea World Drive west off Interstate 5). Seven different 20-minute shows are repeated several times daily. They feature such attractions as Shamu and Baby Shamu, the killer whales, sea lions, whales, and dolphins. In addition, the park has a wide array of special exhibits including marine turtles, whale and dolphin petting pools, a shark viewing area, and penguins. You are encouraged to look at and even touch several whale species. Also noteworthy here are the avian exhibits featuring hundreds of waterfowl from around the world and a new bird show. Be sure to visit the tide pool exhibit where children can pick up bat stars and other marine life. This exhibit provides a good preview of the tide pools you will have a chance to visit on your way up the coast. Sea World is open daily 10:00 a.m. to dusk, with extended hours during summer and holiday periods. Admission is $27.95 for adults, $23.75 for seniors over 55, $19.95 for children 3 to 11, and free for children under 3; (619) 226-3901. Have your hand stamped as you exit and you can return later in the day.

▲▲**Coronado**—Once two islands, Coronado is now a peninsula connected to the mainland by a narrow oceanfront spit. Following your visit to Sea World, return to Interstate 5 southbound and exit to Coronado via the Coronado Bridge. The main attraction here is the century-old Hotel Del Coronado, built in 1888. This Victorian hotel is distinguished by its turrets, tall cupolas, and gingerbread features. The setting for Billy Wilder's *Some Like It Hot*, the hotel is a good place for lunch. You can explore Coronado on a rented bike or go for a paddleboat ride in Mission Bay.

▲**Point Loma**—From Coronado, drive back across the bridge to San Diego and take Harbor Drive west to Rosecrans (S.R. 209). Continue on 209 (it becomes Cañon Street) to Catalina Boulevard. Turn left to Cabrillo National Monument, the Point Loma landmark that commemorates the explorer who claimed this region for Spain in 1542. From this excellent vista point you can see Mexico to the south. There's a small museum at the visitor center. You'll also find a whale lookout where you may spot such cetaceans as gray whales heading south between Christmas and mid-February or heading north on their way back to Alaskan waters in April. The tip-off is the whale's spout or blow, actually a warm breath that condenses into a vapor plume when exhaled into the colder air; a whale blows about three times in a five-minute period. Generally, it surfaces from a cruising depth of 100 feet to take its first breath; then it swims about 20 feet underwater and rises for a second breath; it cruises again and follows a third breath with a deep dive.

Of particular interest are the humpback whales, famed for their musical talents and spectacular manner of leaping into public view.

▲**Stephen Birch Aquarium-Museum**—Continue north on Mission Boulevard through Mission Beach and Pacific Beach to La Jolla. Turn left on La Jolla Boulevard to Prospect Street. Go right on Torrey Pines Road to Expedition Way, and turn right to the museum. With more than 3,000 fish on display, this is America's largest oceanographic exhibit. The interpretive center for the world–famous Scripps Institution of Oceanography, this collection focuses on marine life as well as on earthquakes and weather patterns. Overlooking the beautiful La Jolla coast, the museum features sharks, lionfish, moray eels, octopus and many other species exhibited in 33 tanks. Here you can also learn how waves are created and beaches are formed. The outdoor tidepool plaza is a special treat. This institute complements many of the attractions you saw at Sea World. Open daily 9:00 a.m. to 5:00 p.m. Admission is $6.50 for adults, $5.50 for seniors, $4.50 for children 13 to 17 and $3.50 for children 4 to 12. (619) 534-FISH.

▲▲**Torrey Pines State Park**—Instead of visiting Scripps Aquarium, you may prefer one of the city's fine beaches. Sunbathers and swimmers enjoy La Jolla Shores Beach and Torrey Pines State Park Beach, just north of La Jolla. You reach Torrey Pines by turning left (north) on La Jolla Shores Drive to Torrey Pines Road. Make another left and continue north to the park, located near the golf course. Just beyond this beach is Torrey Pines State Park, one of two places in the state where you'll find natural stands of these gnarled trees. This is one of the finest coastal settings in southern California and a good place for sunbathing and swimming. A fifteen-minute walk south along the beach from Torrey Pines takes you to Black's Beach, known as the area's only nude beach, although not officially sanctioned as such. It's located below some steep cliffs.

▲▲**La Jolla Cove**—An alternative to these beaches is La Jolla Cove, reached by returning south on Torrey Pines

Road to Prospect Street. Turn right and then make another right on Coast Boulevard down to the cove. The beach here is popular with divers, and the adjacent Scripps Park is an ideal place to relax, read, or sunbathe. If you're searching for the California good life, here it is.

▲▲**Prospect Street**—After visiting the cove, stroll along Coast Boulevard to Girard, which will take you back up to Prospect Street, La Jolla's elegant shopping street. Browse in the windows of local realty offices where videos give you a look at homes in the $1 million to $12 million range. Sidewalk vendors sell 14-karat gold jewelry. Stroll past John Cole's Book Shop, located in the historic Wisteria Cottage. This is one of the few bookstores that has its own fireplace. The shop, located at 780 Prospect Street, is open daily except Sunday from 9:30 a.m. to 5:30 p.m. Incidentally, an excellent place for a drink before or after dinner is La Valencia Hotel, a pink palace at 1132 Prospect Street.

▲▲**Mt. Soledad**—After dinner (see suggestions in Day 1), it's time to take in the ultimate San Diego view. Follow La Jolla Boulevard south to Nautilus, turn left and head up to La Jolla Scenic Drive, where you turn left and continue to the summit of Mount Soledad. On the way to the top, you'll pass one of southern California's great social anomalies, hundreds of homes in the $500,000-and-up bracket owned by wealthy Mexican immigrants. The Immigration Service waiting list for Mexicans of limited means who would like to move to California is more than a decade long. But if you have more than $40,000 and are willing to invest it in an American business, it's relatively easy to receive a nonimmigrant visa. This document is generally good for as long as the newcomer remains in business. As a result, Mexican expatriates or those who would like to have residences south and north of the border are welcome after they establish their financial credentials. Like wealthy Italians who look on Swiss border towns as a safe haven for a portion of their assets, these Mexicans see California as their refuge in hard times. This city has attracted more than 300 Mexican millionaire families over the past decade (a recent study shows twenty-eight of these families have invested an estimated $116 million in the local economy). Gazing down at the bougainvillea-covered hillsides, you'll quickly see why. People living here seem to think La Jolla has everything—and they just may be right.

Itinerary Option: Tijuana/Rosarito Beach/Ensenada
Just a half-hour by car from San Diego is one of the world's busiest border towns, Tijuana. The second-largest city on the Pacific Coast of North America, this community of 1.7 million is the jump-off point for the popular resorts of Baja California like Ensenada and Rosarito Beach. For an afternoon or evening of shopping and dining, Tijuana is an excellent choice. Seedy dives have been replaced by a modern cultural center, shopping malls, plazas, and first-class restaurants. Here you can watch bullfights, jai alai, or the races at Agua Caliente Racetrack. Easily reached via the San Diego trolley, or by bus from downtown San Diego, the city is also accessible by car on Interstate 5. Just park at one of the border lots, walk through the customs station, and hail a taxi to the cultural center (agreeing on a price at the outset). The center's museum will give you an overview of the country's history through its Mexican Identities exhibit. Also here are displays on Mexican music, cooking, and heroes like Emiliano Zapata. Inside the ball-shaped Omnimax theater you'll see *People of the Sun*, a film that gives you a glimpse of the Mayan and Aztec pyramids, the famed Copper Canyon train route, and modern resorts like Cancún. The Ballet Folklórico performs each Sunday at the cultural center. During the summer months the Papantla Flyers go through their paces on platforms atop hundred-foot-high poles. For shopping, cross the street to modern Plaza Rio Tijuana, a mall that has everything from Kellogg's Fruti Lupis (Fruit Loops) to Rolex watches at a discount.

You may also enjoy Mexitlan at a cultural theme park at Ocampo and Second streets. Here 150 scale models provide an overview of this nation's pyramids, colonial churches, and contemporary architecture. There are also music and folkloric dance performances, as well as arts and crafts and restaurants. 011-52-531-1112. For more traditional Mexican goods, go downtown on Avenida de la Revolución. Old-timers remember this street as Mexico's attempt to combine Sodom and Gomorrah into a single neighborhood. In years gone by, it was possible to get many things here—including a marriage license and divorce certificate, on the same block. The longest bar in the world, stretching almost the entire distance between Second and Third streets, was a popular hub.

Eager to improve the city's image, the revisionist city fathers have replaced these seedy dives with such downtown clothing shops as Polo Ralph Lauren in Plaza La Jolla at Seventh and Madero and Dorians at Niños Heroes and Second Street. This area is also the logical place to find Mexican arts and crafts. La Fuente, at 921 Avenida de la Revolución in the Condominio Revolución Arcade, has first-class folk art and porcelain goods. A good choice for embroidered dresses and men's *guayabera* shirts is The Emporium at 813 Avenida de la Revolución. Stop in one of the local pharmacies, and you'll be surprised to find American prescription drugs like penicillin sold over the counter along with "cures" for balding and herpes.

For dinner, try one of the city's fine seafood restaurants such as **La Costa** at 150 Calle 7, or take a cab to **Los Arcos**, 201 Escuadron at Boulevard G. Salinas. The Tijuana Convention and Visitors Bureau at 011-52-66-84-04-81 or the Chamber of Commerce at 011-52-66-85-84-72 can provide additional information. Baja Reservations can provide hotel information for this region. (619) 222-9099.

A pleasant alternative to the hectic border atmosphere of Tijuana is Baja's Pacific Coast. Rosarito Beach is just half an hour away and you can continue along the Pacific on the beautiful highway to Ensenada. Fine beaches, moderately priced resorts and restaurants are the primary attraction. If you're driving your own vehicle buy Mexican auto insurance from one of the companies located at the border. Some rental cars can be taken into

Mexico. Check with Tijuana & Baja Information at (619) 299-8518 for more information and hotel reservations. Or call the Tijuana Convention and Tourism Bureau at (619) 298-4105.

The oceanfront **Rosarito Beach Hotel**, (800) 343-8582 or 011-52-66-12-11-06, is easily reached by taking the Mexico 1-D tollway 15 miles south from Tijuana. There's a pleasant dining room overlooking the Pacific, and you can enjoy a roomy suite for about $59 to $99. Continue south about 20 minutes along the coast to Puerto Nuevo, a village of 2,000 where 46 restaurants serve up the local specialty, fresh lobster burritos. Try **Ortega's** overlooking the Pacific.

Sixty miles south of Tijuana is Ensenada, a major Pacific port where you'll find excellent seafood. **El Rey Sol** restaurant, 011-52-66-678-1733, at **Lopez Mateos** and **Avenida Blancarte** is a good choice for upscale dining. Or simply visit the wharf area where local stands serve up fresh seafood tacos. Six miles south of Ensenada on Mexico 1 is Estero Beach Resort where rooms run $52 to $90 a night. 011-52-66-676-6225.

DISNEYLAND

If you've been there, Disneyland needs no introduction. If you haven't, the Eighth Wonder of the World, America's first theme park, will likely exceed all expectations. There is a great deal to see and enjoy at Disneyland, but the crowds are big and so are the lines. Fortunately, the park is also a place where a bit of strategy will make this day a memorable one. Just hum a few bars of "Zippity Doo Dah," and you're on your way.

Suggested Schedule	
8:00 a.m.	Drive north on Interstate 5.
10:00 a.m.	Arrive at Disneyland.
11:30 a.m.	Lunch.
2:00 p.m.	Check into your hotel, swim, relax.
4:00 p.m.	Return to Disneyland.
5:30 p.m.	Dinner.
Evening	Disneyland under the stars.

Travel Route: San Diego to Anaheim (95 miles)
From San Diego, take Interstate 5 north to the Harbor Boulevard exit in Anaheim. Follow the signs west to the Disneyland entrance at 1313 Harbor Boulevard.

Disneyland
Since it opened in 1955, "The Happiest Place on Earth" has changed the face of the amusement park industry. Tired of taking his own children to seedy thrill palaces run by sloppy employees and rude roustabouts, Walt Disney decided to create a healthy family environment under the spiritual leadership of his own animated off-spring. Although many of the standards Disney set at this park now extend throughout the theme park industry, it is important to recognize some of the ideas he pioneered here. To differentiate from its predecessors, the amusement park nomenclature was changed.

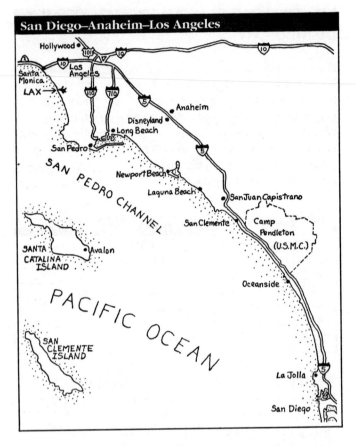

San Diego–Anaheim–Los Angeles

The more than 9,000 employees are trained to serve as a park "cast," making a visit to "wardrobe" before going "on stage" at Disneyland. Rudeness is forbidden: an employee who is surly or insults a guest will be fired on the spot. There is no visible trash at the 76-acre park, because of the vigilance of cleaning crews in this environment where the half-life of a piece of litter seems to be about one minute. Workers happily repaint the shooting gallery once a day, wipe dew off benches, chlorinate the submarine lagoon, change light bulbs at least one month before they are expected to burn out, and repaint everything in one of 2,000 officially designated park hues. Flowers are always in bloom here; that's because most of them are in boxes, not in the ground. This way more than 1,000 new flowers can bloom on the Disneyland grounds every day.

The park is famous for its long lines. Picnic lunches are forbidden and the P.A. system can get to you. But with a little bit of planning, the park can be a lot of fun. Mid-week, nonholiday visits are always the best. Whenever you come, a few basic strategies are good to keep in mind. The sooner you can arrive, the better. If you can leave San Diego a little ahead of our suggested schedule, the morning lines may be shorter. Eat ahead of the regular meal hour, beating lines at the food stands. Take a break in the midafternoon when park traffic peaks. Choose your rides by category. For example, the Matterhorn Bobsleds and Big Thunder Mountain are very similar experiences: ride one and you can skip the other. There really isn't enough time in one day to stand in line for both Star Tours and Space Mountain: choose the one that sounds best to you. It's also possible to have a lot of fun in some of the stationary attractions. When the ride lines seem too long, head for Tom Sawyer Island, the Swiss Family Tree House, or Main Street. Save at least one or two major attractions for evening when you'll find lines diminished.

Summer hours: Generally open every day 8:00 a.m. to 1:00 a.m.; however, the park does occasionally close early at 10:00 p.m.

Winter hours (September to June): Open every day 10:00 a.m. to 6:00 p.m., 9:00 a.m. to midnight Saturdays and Sundays. To verify park hours and get more information, please call (714) 999-4565 so you won't end up shut out like Chevy Chase at Wally World in *National Lampoon's Vacation* Admission to Disneyland and a pass for all rides costs $31.00 for adults and $25.00 for children ages 3 to 11.

Sightseeing Highlights
At Disneyland there are no "rides," only "adventures" and "attractions." Here are some of the best:
▲▲▲**Star Tours (Tomorrowland)**—One of the most

imaginative new rides to be found at any amusement park. A flight simulator takes you on a hair-raising trip to the Moon of Endor. The running gag here is that nearly everything that can go wrong on a trip to outer space does. Star Tours, actually a fly-by-night carrier, is breaking in a droid pilot named Rex (his voice is provided by Pee Wee Herman) on this trip. How this klutz got by the FAA is a complete mystery. The entire trip appears to take place in a celestial minefield as the ship is rocked by everything from frozen ice fragments to laser blasts.

▲▲**Captain EO (Tomorrowland)**—Here's the perfect attraction for someone who's never had a chance to see 3-D. This 17-minute short subject directed by Francis Ford Coppola (George Lucas is the executive producer) stars famed moon walker Michael Jackson as the Captain. The musical space fantasy comes complete with smoke, lights, and laser effects that explode into the 700-seat theater. The Disney organization is proud that no one leaves the theater with a headache, a common complaint from 3-D audiences of 30 years ago.

▲▲**Space Mountain (Tomorrowland)**—No one does dark rides better than Disney, as this roller coaster trip through the cosmos proves. Your rocket trip begins at a NASA-like space station. Here you whirl among the stars on a space vehicle. The effect is kind of like careening around the dome of a planetarium at 80 miles per hour. Meteor showers make the ride memorable. Not for the faint of heart.

▲▲**Matterhorn Bobsleds (Fantasyland)**—Thanks to the waterfalls, glacial lakes, and mountain scenery, this is an entertaining roller coaster ride that feels like sliding through the Alps. Four-passenger sleds on two different runs wind in and out of the artificial peak. No real steep drops here, just a lot of fast fun.

▲**It's A Small World (Fantasyland)**—Originally designed for the 1964 New York World's Fair, this trip carries passengers by boat through the 1,400-foot-long Seven Seaways, featuring 297 miniature model children of 100 nations who sing about the virtues of world

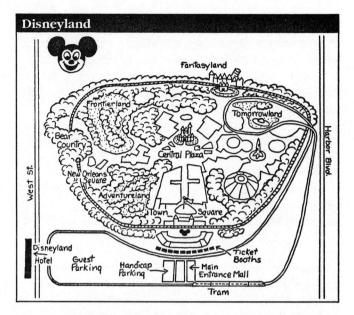

Disneyland

friendship. This extremely popular attraction goes over big with kids, though some adults find it like swallowing a bottle of saccharin.

▲**Peter Pan (Fantasyland)**—The ideal place for those who are philosophically opposed to growing up, this aerial fantasy ride takes you deep into the heart of the Peter Pan syndrome.

▲▲**Alice in Wonderland (Fantasyland)**—The best of the dark rides for children. Many of Lewis Carroll's memorable characters are found here.

▲▲▲**Tom Sawyer Island (Frontierland)**—Linked with the mainland by raft, this is perfect for kids and a welcome break from the ride lines. On this island, youngsters enjoy crawling through tunnels, forts, and mining shafts, playing on a teeter-totter rock, or running across the barrel bridge. The island is also a fine place for parents to rest because it's impossible to lose kids unless they decide to sneak back to the mainland alone.

▲▲▲**Fantasmic (Frontierland)**—This blend of pyrotechnics, lasers, fog, fiber optics, music, and 51 live performers is a special presentation offered three times each evening. The 22-minute show is staged around the Cider Mill on Tom Sawyer's Island. Stand along the banks of Disneyland's Rivers of America in Frontierland and New Orleans Square to see this show. A full cast of Disney characters appears in this fantasy tale. It runs all summer long and whenever the park is open in the evening.

▲Big Thunder Mountain Railroad (Frontierland)—A thrill ride through a star-crossed western mining district. The train dodges slides, bats, floods, and other perils. Serious roller coaster buffs will find this one relatively tame.

▲Splash Mountain (Critter Country)—This log-flume thrill ride, lasting nearly 10 minutes, takes guests through caverns in a mountain that soars 87 feet above the Orange County landscape. As guests float through the mountain caverns they watch characters from "Song of the South" enact the adventures of Brer Rabbit as he tries to elude Brer Fox and Brer Bear. The ride includes five drops including one in the dark. The final 47-degree plunge takes you down into the Briar Patch. Waits are often lengthy for this popular attraction.

▲Country Bear Vacation Hoedown (Critter Country)—Here's a chance to see Disney's patented Audio-Animatronics that synchronizes voice and body movements to give animated objects lifelike qualities. This comical music show presented in the Country Bear Playhouse is good for children as well as adults who enjoy listening to the antics of 18 bears, a raccoon, a buffalo, a stag, and a moose. A Country Bear Christmas Special is presented from Thanksgiving through New Year's Day.

▲Pirates of the Caribbean (New Orleans Square)— This trip begins with a ride past the Blue Bayou restaurant on a flat-bottom bateau. Suddenly you plunge down a waterfall, pass through pirate caves and into the midst of an all-out war. You see fighting, plundering, looting, shooting, and a wench auction.

▲▲Haunted Mansion (New Orleans Square)—It took a decade to create this spookhouse. An elevator ride takes you down to doom buggies that lead past hordes of Disney terrorists. The holographic special effects do an excellent job of raising the dead.

▲▲**Mickey's Toontown** is full of characters straight from Disney's animated classic. Here's your chance to chat with talkative manholes, fire hydrants or spinning flowers. You can visit Mickey's red-shingled home, Goofy's Bounce House and Chip and Dale's home perched in an acorn tree. Stay awhile and you'll probably feel like you've been cast in a cartoon.

▲▲▲**Electrical Light Parade (Main Street)**—During the summer, this extravaganza is staged nightly at 8:50 and 11:00. Brilliantly lit floats feature all the familiar Disney characters. Many of the performers are decked out in lights. My preference is for the 8:50 p.m. parade because it's capped by a major fireworks display. The pyrotechnics are ignited by the flight of the pixie Tinker Bell, who soars above Disneyland waving her magic wand. Incidentally, two to four daytime parades are also offered at the park. Check the times when you enter.

Lodging

Anaheim offers a variety of hotel rooms in all price ranges. Since you're only going to have one day at the park, I suggest taking a hotel within walking distance. Check in during your midafternoon break, relax or swim, and then walk or take a convenient shuttle over from the hotel. Reservations are always a good idea on weekends, in the summer, and during holiday periods. In the luxury category ($150 a night and up) are **Disneyland Hotel**, 1150 West Cerritos Avenue, 92802, (714) 778-6600, and the **Anaheim Marriott**, 700 West Convention Way, 92802, (800) 62-MOUSE or (714) 750-8000. Moderately priced hotels ($50-$90) include the **Best Western Anaheim Inn**, 1630 South Harbor Boulevard, 92802, (800) 854-8175 or (714) 774-1050, and **Travelodge Park South**, 2171 South Harbor Boulevard, 92802, (800) 922-3879 or (714) 750-3100. Budget hotels include **Zaby's Motor Lodge**, 444 West Katella Avenue, 92802, and **Sandman Inn**, 921 South Harbor Boulevard, 92802, (714) 999-0684.

Fullerton Hacienda Youth Hostel, at 1700 North Harbor Boulevard, Fullerton 92635, offers beds at $13.50 per night. Call (714) 738-3721 to confirm space availability.

Campers: At **Vacationland**, 1343 West Street, 92802, (714) 774-2267, sites rent for $28 to $37 per night; across from Disneyland. **Travelers World RV Park**, 333 West Ball Road, 92805, (714) 991-0100, has sites for $17.50 to $22 per night. Located 1.5 miles from Disneyland.

Food

Because of the long lines for Disneyland attractions, I suggest taking your meals at the park. The **Blue Bayou** is a pleasant sit-down establishment in New Orleans Square, but the food is not worth the typically long wait (reservations are not accepted). In the interest of enjoying as many rides as possible, I favor establishments with shorter lines. Probably the best restaurant in the park, besides **The 31** (a private club), is the **Tahitian Terrace** in Adventureland. You may find it more convenient to settle for Disney fast food. Don't worry too much about shopping around: the Nottinghamburgers in Fantasyland and the Spaceburgers in Tomorrowland all come from the same central freezer. Eat in advance of normal meal hours to avoid long lines on busy days. Another possibility is to take the Monorail over to the Disneyland Hotel where a variety of restaurants and fast-food establishments may provide quicker service than park facilities on a busy day.

Helpful Hint

The Anaheim Chamber of Commerce is at 100 South Anaheim Boulevard, Suite 300, Anaheim 92805, (714) 758-0222.

LOS ANGELES

A city that contributes handsomely to America's imaginative life, Los Angeles has a laid-back image that belies its industriousness. Great streams of traffic roar past well-preserved sanctuaries of the dinosaur age. Today you will join that stream as you make your way north to one of the studios. You may have a chance to watch a movie being made, become part of a television audience, or visit a theme park that lets you participate in the film-making process. Then you'll visit one of the West's great libraries, see an architectural gem, and, if time permits, stroll through a museum dedicated to the Southwest.

Suggested Schedule

8:30 a.m.	Leave Anaheim.
9:30 a.m.	Arrive at Warner, Universal, or NBC studios.
2:00 p.m.	If you chose the Warner Bros. or NBC studios tour, continue to the Huntington Gardens in San Marino, Gamble House in Pasadena, and/or Southwest Museum/Lummis House in Los Angeles.
Balance of day.	At leisure with dinner at Musso and Frank, Canter's, or the Original Pantry.

Los Angeles

Although now as famous for its smog as it once was for its orange groves, this remains a city of great beauty. Rimmed by mountains to the north and an ocean to the west and south, L.A.'s Moorish residential neighborhoods, great parks, and seemingly endless freeways provide the kind of contrasts that make California a source of continuing fascination. From its beginning, Los Angeles has been a melting pot. The city's first census in the eighteenth century found a kind of Heinzian variety among its eleven pioneer families. Thanks to miscegenation, early Los Angeles could count Negro-Mulatto, Spanish-Indian, Mestizo-Mulatto, and Indian-Mulatto families within its ranks. While San Francisco came to life as the port of entry for the gold rush of 1849, Los Angeles remained essentially a farming town. The city lacked the bare essentials of urban growth, such as a decent port. Oceangoing vessels had to anchor out in deep water and transfer cargo to smaller boats that braved the tricky tides and wind. In the late nineteenth century, humiliated residents had to vote a $600,000 subsidy to persuade Southern Pacific President Charles Crocker to bring his railroad into Los Angeles via the San Fernando Valley. Los Angeles was also a desert, 200 miles from the nearest tributary.

A small group of businessmen including General Moses Sherman, Harrison Gray Otis, Eli Clark, Isaias Hellman, H.K.S. O'Melveny, and Otto Brant saw the city's potential. Farmers were lured from the Midwest with posters of knee-high squash and grapefruits the size of pumpkins. When water grew short, the Los Angeles pioneers turned verdant regions like the Owens Valley to dust as they diverted the Owens River hundreds of miles south to their own backyard. A new port was created and geologists uncovered vast local oil reserves. As the birthplace of the movie industry, the aerospace industry, and the freeway, Los Angeles emerged as one of the world's leading year-round tourist destinations. And why not? Where else can you spend the morning gawking at the homes of stars and the afternoon sitting in their studio audiences? Say good-bye to the Magic Kingdom, put your convertible on cruise control, and you're ready to see it for yourself.

Studio Tours

All three of the studios recommended below are within a few minutes of each other. Because the Universal Studios tour takes five and a half hours, you won't have time to do it and the Warner Bros. visit in the same day. But if you get an early start at NBC (9:00 a.m.), you'll have a chance to pick up show tickets, enjoy the tour, and make it over to Universal by 11:00 a.m.

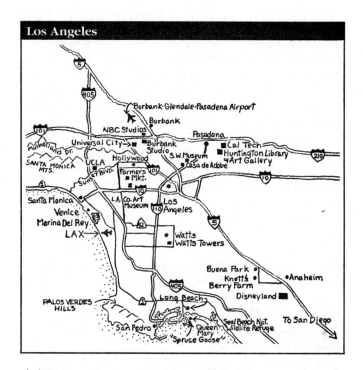

▲▲**Warner Bros. V.I.P. Tour**, 4000 Warner Boulevard, (818) 954-1744. It's harder than ever these days to see how products are created. The tour of Ford's incomparable Rouge Works in Detroit is now closed to the public. And because of liability problems, it's pretty tough to get inside a meat packing plant or a refinery. Hollywood also used to pride itself on backstage tours. Even when business was slow at places such as the MGM lot, studio executives would send trucks scurrying around to create the illusion that films were in production. Today it is possible to be part of a television show audience or take a theme park-type ride through a studio tourist attraction (see below). But only one motion picture studio makes its entire operation accessible to the public.

The home of Warner Bros. Pictures runs a V.I.P. tour worthy of its name. This two-hour trip takes you backstage, on sets, and into the wardrobe department and vast prop room. You can watch actors blow their lines, see a director stomp his foot, and, with luck, grab some autographs. Here it is even possible to enjoy a studio perk: lunch in the commissary.

From the days of early silent movie stars like Douglas Fairbanks to contemporary celebrities like Steve Martin, this 100-acre location has been the Burbank branch of the Hollywood dream. When producers of *Cannery Row* found the Monterey site too dolled up for their liking a few years back, they re-created it here. And why not? With a vast back lot, 39 stages, shops, foundries, and a property department that uses enough lumber in set construction to create 200 three-bedroom houses each year, this studio can meet just about any production company's requirements. As you might expect in any self-respecting Hollywood studio, there is a jungle here as well as streets that can be made up to look like skid row, New York, or Paris. History buffs will be particularly impressed by the Warner Bros.' $24-million prop room. Stored here is Big Bertha, the 300,000-pound chandelier used in *Funny Lady*. Also gathering dust are the furnishings from Rick's Café in *Casablanca*. If you time your visit right, you will have a good chance of going on set and watching live performances. But be forewarned: the pace is slow.

Filmmaking is a painstaking art. It takes an entire 12-hour workday to get two minutes of usable film for a feature-length movie. (A television set is slightly more productive, averaging seven or eight minutes of film per day.) Operated by Warner Bros. between 1927 and 1972, the studio had 7,000 employees at its peak. Few kings had more power than the company's first and last emperor, Jack Warner. "He was in absolute control," recalls Dick Mason, a former Warner secretary who manages the tour and begins the two-hour visit with background information on the stars. "He would pick up the phone and you were hired or fired off that call." Tours are conducted at 9:00 a.m. and 4:30 p.m. weekdays. Three additional tours are added during the summer season. The tour costs $27 and reservations are required. Children under 10 are not allowed. Lunch in the lot's commissary is possible on a space available basis.

▲**NBC Studios**—3000 West Alameda Avenue, Burbank 91523. (818) 840-3537. If you've longed to stand in Vanna White's parking spot, this tour is for you. A $6 one-hour visit ($6 for seniors, $3.75 for youths 5-14) gives you a chance to see how shows are produced. You'll have a chance to step inside the ministudio equipped with a simulated control booth and participate in a brief simulated game show production. The special effects set gives some guests a chance to fly Superman-style over Los Angeles. The tour continues through the wardrobe department, set construction facility, "The Tonight Show," and a news studio. The NBC Peacock Store adjacent to the studio is a convenient place to buy specialty merchandise and mementos of popular shows. Groups can take a special children's tour, a seminar on how television works, a mystery soap-opera trip, or combine their studio visit with stops at famous Hollywood spots like Mann's Chinese Theater.

The studio will not mail show tickets beyond a 150-mile radius. You will only be able to book ahead if you have a friend or relative near Los Angeles willing to correspond in your behalf. If you live beyond the 150-mile limit, request a guest letter that may be exchanged for tickets at the studio on a space-available basis. (This letter does not guarantee you a seat.) With or without the guest letter, the best plan is to arrive as early as possible at the ticket counter located in the Guest Relations Office. You'll find the ticket counter on the west side of the building off California and Olive streets. Determined visitors often line up well before the ticket counter opens at 8:00 a.m. weekdays and 10:00 a.m. weekends. Many of them are seeking "The Tonight Show" tickets, distributed only on the day of the show and limited to two per person.

The L.A. Convention and Visitors Bureau offers a free guide to TV tapings. Write or stop by one of its visitor information centers. Minimum ages for admittance to these shows range from 9 to 16. For information on ticket availability and tours, call or write the studio.

▲▲**Universal Studios Hollywood**—Located off

the Hollywood Freeway at the Universal Center or Lankershim Boulevard exit, Universal Studios is the world's largest motion picture and television production facility. (818) 508-9600. Unlike at Warner Studios, you won't have a chance to see current filming on sets. Instead, the narrated tram tour through the 420-acre front and back lots offers an encounter with King Kong, a chance to meet marine mammals like Jaws, and see the parting of the Red Sea. You'll also enjoy visiting the Special Effects Stage, which offers an inside look at movie making magic. Volunteers help reenact scenes from films like *E.T.* A highlight of the tour is the simulated 8.8 earthquake. This two-minute catastrophe drops the tram into a seismic holocaust and triggers a flash flood. Hopefully, this is as close as you'll ever get to the real thing.

Before or after your tram tour, there'll be a chance to enjoy other park attractions such as a Miami Vice Action Spectacular that features 50 live stunts and special effects. The Star Trek Adventure gives visitors a chance to appear in an original featurette. Footage shot here is intercut with film from the series, and then turned into a seven-minute short instantly available on videocassette. The Backdraft attraction is also popular. In the entertaining stunt show performers endure bottles broken over their heads and survive 30-foot-high falls. Universal Studios Hollywood is open daily except Thanksgiving and Christmas. During summer and holiday periods, tours run from 9:00 a.m. to 5:00 p.m. From July 1 through August 21, hours are extended from 7:00 a.m. to 5:00 p.m. In the off-season, the hours are 10:00 a.m. to 3:30 p.m. weekdays and 9:30 a.m. to 3:30 p.m. weekends. Admission is $31 for adults and $24.95 for seniors and children ages 3 to 11. Children under 3 enter free.

Helpful Hint
Free show tickets are available from Paramount Promotional Services at 860 N. Gower Street, Hollywood 90038. (213) 956-5575.

Other Sightseeing Highlights
**▲▲The Huntington Library, Art Collections, and
Botanical Gardens**—Collis Huntington was one of
California's Big Four railroad pioneers who monopolized
commercial transport within the state during the late
nineteenth century. Following his death, Collis's second
wife, Arabella, married his nephew and business associ-
ate, Henry Huntington. After selling off his controlling
interest in the Southern Pacific, Huntington pioneered the
Pacific Electric Railway Co., the major streetcar line in Los
Angeles. In San Marino he built one of California's finest
estates. Today scholars from around the world come to
visit the Huntington Library, which houses over 500,000
books including a rare Gutenberg Bible and Ben
Franklin's handwritten autobiography. The former
Huntington mansion is now an art gallery focused on
eighteenth- and nineteenth-century British art, tapestries
and sculpture. Among the famed paintings in this collection is Gainsborough's *Blue Boy*.

The entire complex is surrounded by gardens where
you'll find plants in bloom year-round. For instance, in
the North Vista, you'll see seventeenth-century Italian
statues bordering a lawn surrounded by azaleas and
camellias. The Rose Garden features hundreds of varieties, including America's largest collection of tea roses.
The Japanese Garden is actually a five-acre landscaped
canyon that includes a furnished Japanese house and a
Zen garden. Best of all is the 12-acre desert garden,
which embraces the largest outdoor desert plant collection in the world.

Open Tuesday through Sunday 1:00 p.m. to 4:30 p.m.
Garden tours are conducted Tuesday through Friday at
1:00 p.m. You need reservations on Sunday unless one
member of your group lives outside Los Angeles County.
The Huntington is located at 1151 Oxford Road, (818)
405-2100. Closed on holidays. A $2 donation is requested.
▲▲Gamble House—Designed by Charles and Henry
Greene, this is a classic piece of Craftsman design built
for the heirs to the Procter & Gamble fortune in 1908.

Built for $50,000, its sculptured woodwork, Japanese overtones, Tiffany glass panels, and beautiful grounds make this bungalow one of the most visited homes in the area. It's in perfect condition and now belongs to the University of Southern California's architecture school. Hour-long tours are offered Tuesday through Sunday from noon to 3:00 p.m. Closed holidays. Admission is $4 for adults, $2 for college students, and free for visitors under 12. It's located at 4 Westmoreland Place off North Orange Grove Boulevard, Pasadena. (818) 793-3334.

▲▲**Southwest Museum/Lummis House**—Educated at Harvard, Charles Lummis made history by quitting his job on a Cincinnati newspaper in 1885 and walking to Los Angeles. His account of the journey, published in newspapers coast to coast, made him in an instant celebrity. As he strolled across America, large crowds showed up along the route to greet this happy wanderer. The day after his arrival in southern California, he was hired as the first city editor of the *Los Angeles Times*. Round-the-clock shifts led to a stroke and, after convalescing in New Mexico, he returned to Los Angeles to become the first city librarian, editor of *Sunset* magazine, and author of numerous books. His home, at 200 East Avenue 43, at the west corner of Carlota Boulevard, is headquarters of the Historical Society of Southern California and a museum. Designed by Lummis, the building is open Thursday through Sunday 1:00 p.m. to 4:00 p.m. Closed holidays. (213) 222-0546. Lummis also founded the nearby Southwest Museum at 234 Museum Drive, north of the intersection with Marmion Way in Highland Park. Here you will find arts and crafts from Alaska to Mexico and galleries that focus on artifacts from the Southwest, the Plains, California, and the Northwest Coast. Open Tuesday through Sunday 11:00 a.m. to 5:00 p.m. Closed holidays. Admission is $4 for adults, $2 for seniors and students, and $1 for youths 7 to 18. (213) 221-2163.

Itinerary Option: Pasadena
Beautiful Victorian, craftsman, Mediterranean, and Tudor architecture, grand art museums, and a meticu-

lously restored resort hotel make Pasadena a great place for casual touring. The **Norton Simon Museum** at Colorado and North Orange Grove boulevards has an outstanding collection of European and Asian masters. In addition to the classic works by such artists as Rembrandt, Rubens, Raphael, Botticelli, Cézanne, Goya, and Toulouse-Lautrec, there's a beautiful sculpture garden showcasing the works of Rodin and Henry Moore. The museum is open Thursday through Sunday from noon to 6:00 p.m. Admission is $4 for adults and $2 for students. Children under 12 are admitted free. (818) 449-6840.

Stop by the Pasadena Housing and Community Development office at City Hall, 100 North Garfield Avenue to pick up a self-guided auto tour of the Pasadena region. Among the 73 highlights on this tour are Descanso Gardens, Hastings Ranch, and the famous Pasadena Playhouse where many Hollywood stars got their start. You'll also enjoy visiting the Ritz Carlton Huntington Hotel located in the midst of a parklike 20-acre setting at 1401 South Oak Knoll Avenue. It's in the heart of the beautiful Hillcrest neighborhood. (818) 568-3900.

Lodging

Near downtown is the **Eastlake Inn**, an 1887 Victorian house at 1442 Kellam Avenue, 90026; rooms run $65 to $150. **Salisbury House** near downtown in the West Adams District is a handsome craftsman home. This B&B at 2773 West 20th Street, Los Angeles 90018, offers rooms ranging from $75 to $100. (213) 737-7817 or (800) 373-1778.

Hotel Del Capri at 10587 Wilshire Boulevard in Westwood is convenient to the UCLA campus. Rates range from $85 to $120. (310) 474-3511.

In the Beverly Hills area, the **Beverly Terrace Hotel** at 469 North Doheny Drive, 90210, has rooms starting at $55. (310) 274-8141. The **Beverly Rodeo Hotel** at 360 North Rodeo Drive, Beverly Hills 90210, is in the midst of boutique row. Rooms start at $140. (310) 273-0300.

For total luxury, try the **Hotel Bel-Air** at 701 Stone Canyon Road in Beverly Hills. Rooms run $285 to $435 in a parklike setting. (310) 472-1211.

The **Marina del Rey Hotel**, five miles north of Los Angeles International Airport and surrounded on three sides by water, is convenient to the beach. $125 to $210. It's located at 13534 Bali Way, Marina del Rey 90292. (800) 882-4000 outside California, (800) 862-7462 inside California. (310) 301-1000. Also close to the water is the **Venice Beach House** at 15 30th Avenue, Venice 90251. Rooms including breakfast run around $80 to $150. (310) 823-1966.

Channel Road Bed and Breakfast at 219 West Channel Road, Santa Monica 90402, offers oceanview rooms in a colonial revival from $85 to $195. (310) 459-1920. Another possibility is the art deco **Shangri-La Hotel** at 1301 Ocean Avenue, Santa Monica 90401. Units run from $110 to $230. (310) 394-2791. The **Best Western Santa Monica Gateway** has rooms from $69 to $99. It's located at 1920 Santa Monica Boulevard, Santa Monica 90404. (310) 829-9100.

Bed and Breakfast of Los Angeles at 3924 East 14th Street, Long Beach 90804, provides rooms in private homes beginning at $40. (310) 493-6837.

A number of youth hostels in the Los Angeles area offer accommodations in the $12 to $15 range. The **Hollywood YMCA Youth Hostel** at 1553 North Hudson Avenue, Hollywood 90028, is open year-round. (213) 467-4161. Over 18 only. The **Los Angeles International Hostel** at 3601 South Gaffey Street, Building 613, San Pedro 90731, is open in the summer. (310) 831-8109. It's located 20 miles from downtown Los Angeles. The 200-bed **Santa Monica International Hostel** at 1436 Second Street is the largest on the West Coast. It also preserves and encircles the city's oldest structure, the Rapp Saloon. It costs just $16 to $25 to stay at this coastal hostel where the average hotel room runs $75. (310) 393-9913. Campers should refer to Anaheim suggestions, Day 3.

Food

In downtown Los Angeles, the **Original Pantry**, at 877 South Figueroa Street, is a landmark known for its generous portions. A good place for a steak, very popular at breakfast. Open 24 hours. Always busy, but the wait is worth it. Inexpensive. (213) 972-9279. **Canter's on Fairfax Restaurant, Delicatessen, and Bakery** at 419 North Fairfax is a place to forget about the Pritikin diet. The waitresses here are great. (Marsha Francis of *The Paper*, a West Hollywood weekly, tells about a customer here who ordered a Coke only to be advised by the waitress that she should switch to Pepsi because it was a larger bottle for the same money.) Inexpensive. (213) 651-2030. **Musso and Frank Grill**, another local classic, at 6667 Hollywood Boulevard, has been around since 1919. (213) 467-7788. Moderate to expensive American fare. The moderately priced **Angeli Caffè** at 7274 Melrose Avenue in Los Angeles is a good choice for pizza. (213) 936-9086. In Koreatown, try **Arunee**, an inexpensive spot at 853 S. Vermont Avenue. (213) 385-6653. The food at **Spago**, Wolfgang Puck's expensive restaurant at 1114 Horn Avenue, West Hollywood, is almost as well known as some of the celebrities who dine there. (213) 652-4025. For French cooking, try **Tulipe Bistro** at 8360 Melrose Ave. (213) 655-7400. Another good bet is **City** at 180 S. La Brea Avenue. (213) 938-2155. The international menu includes Thai, Indian, Korean, Greek, Japanese, Italian, and American dishes. Their version of the Hostess cupcake puts the original to shame. One of the city's finest French restaurants is **Citrus** at 6703 Melrose Avenue. (213) 857-0034. Chef-owner Michael Richard is known for his seafood specialties and his whimsy. If you're searching for coffee, cake, or pasta salad, try **Java** at 7286 Beverly Boulevard. (213) 931-4943. An inexpensive choice for lunch in Pasadena is **Birdies Café and Muffinery** at 17 South Raymond Avenue. (818) 449-5884. Also in Pasadena, try the innovative Sino-Mediterranean cuisine at **Ciao Yie,** at 54 West Colorado Boulevard. (818) 578-1231.

Nightlife

The ultimate Southern California entertainment experience is the **Hollywood Bowl.** On a warm night, you'll
find this romantic setting a great place to catch the stars
under the stars. Join 17,000 of your closest friends at
2301 North Highland Avenue. (213) 850-2000. **The
Palace**, a converted theater, offers dancing to rock 'n'
roll downstairs and jazz upstairs. It's at 1735 North Vine
Street. (213) 467-4571. Another good choice is the **Vine
Street Bar and Grill** at 1610 North Vine Street in
Hollywood. Italian food is served at this jazz club. (213)
463-4375. For comedy, try **Improvisation** at 8162
Melrose, (213) 651-2583), or the **Comedy Store,** 8433
West Sunset Boulevard. (213) 656-6225.

Helpful Hints

The Los Angeles Information Center is at 695 South
Figueroa, between Wilshire and Seventh, open 8:30 a.m.
to 5:00 p.m. Monday through Friday, (213) 624-7300.
Their mailing address is 515 S. Figueroa, 11th floor, Los
Angeles 90071. Or call the 24–hour visitor hotline (213)
689-8822. For the latest details on music, art, dance,
theater and festival, call (213) 688-ARTS.

Itinerary Options

Knott's Berry Farm—Located in Buena Park just 15
minutes from Disneyland, this was southern California's
original theme park. Built around a Wild West theme, it
has thrill rides, a Snoopy play area for kids, rapids, one
of the best log rides in California, regular shoot-outs (the
undertaker comes four or five times a day), holdups,
and shorter lines than its Anaheim competitor. XK-1, a
participatory flight ride gives pilots a chance to do barrel
rolls, dives, climbs, and even to fly upside down. If you
have an extra day, by all means try Knott's. Located at
8039 Beach Boulevard, (714) 220-5200. Open daily
except Christmas. From Memorial Day to Labor Day, the
park is open Sunday through Friday from 10:00 a.m. to
midnight and Saturday from 10:00 a.m. to 1:00 a.m.
During the balance of the year, Knott's is open Monday

through Friday 10:00 a.m. to 6:00 p.m., Saturday 10:00 a.m. to 10:00 p.m., and Sunday 10:00 a.m. to 7:00 p.m. Admission is $28.50 for adults, and $18.50 for seniors and ages 3 to 11.

Queen Mary—A self-guided tour takes you through this luxurious ocean liner berthed in Long Beach. You can dine here and, if you really like the ship, spend the night in one of the cabins. Admission is $8. Open year-round 10:00 a.m. to 6:00 p.m., but the box office closes at 5:00 p.m. Extended hours from June 22 to Labor Day. Call before visiting. (213) 435-3511.

Optional Extension: Catalina

Santa Catalina is one of the few places in southern California where a car won't do you much good. But if you're ready to walk or sail, and if you enjoy fishing, biking, swimming, or backpacking, then head on over. Nearly 90 percent wilderness, this 76-square-mile retreat has more buffalo than condos. Docking at the romantic port of Avalon after a two-hour ferry ride from Los Angeles, you can see that Catalina got lost somewhere on the way to the late twentieth century. Mansions like the Holly Hill House—a Queen Anne with a cupola, cone-shaped roof, and portholes for windows—suggest a kind of "Pasadena-by-the-Sea." But as you walk along Avalon Harbor into downtown, it becomes obvious that Catalina is that rarest of places, a family-style resort where honeymooners, backpackers, deep-sea fishermen, school groups, and sailors can get comfortably lost.

If you're looking for restaurants with wine stewards named Pierre or hotels with 40-foot-high fountains, Catalina may be a disappointment. Its siren call is for people who appreciate the best deep-sea fishing, love to dive in protected coves, or take their bird-watching seriously. You could spend weeks exploring Catalina's 54 miles of coastline by launch, pulling into secluded gems like Little Harbor and Fourth of July Cove. While the ocean here is on the cool side, divers and snorkelers flock in to take advantage of the excellent underwater visibility.

To reach Catalina from terminals in Long Beach or San Pedro, reserve space on Catalina Cruises by calling (800) 228-2546. Additional service is provided by Catalina Express from San Pedro, Long Beach, and Redondo Beach. (213) 519-1212. Many visitors go for the day, but you might consider spending the night in Avalon. Hotel rooms (tight on weekends and during the summer months) are available by calling Catalina Visitor's Information Center at (310) 510-2000 or (in California) (800) 4-AVALON. Among the lodging available here is the **Zane Grey Inn**, the writer's former home, where rooms run $55 to $125, depending on the season. It's located at 199 Chime Tower Road. (310) 510-0966. Across the street from the beach, the **Pavilion Lodge** at 513 Crescent Avenue, (310) 510-1788, offers rooms from $49 to $158, also depending on the season. The oceanfront **Hotel Villa Portofino** at 111 Crescent Avenue runs $52 to $225. (310) 510-0555. Located in Two Harbors, the **Banning House Lodge** is a great retreat in a remote setting. (310) 510-0303. Expensive.

LOS ANGELES TO SANTA BARBARA

Looking at prehistoric Los Angeles and then seeing the splendors of Beverly Hills and Will Rogers's old ranch will get your day off to a nice start. Then it's time to enjoy the opulent J. Paul Getty Museum, designed like an ancient Roman villa. A drive up the Malibu Coast takes you to Ventura and tonight's resting place, Santa Barbara.

Suggested Schedule

9:30 a.m.	La Brea Tar Pits.
11:00 a.m.	Beverly Hills.
1:30 p.m.	Will Rogers State Park.
3:00 p.m.	Getty Museum.
5:00 p.m.	Drive to Santa Barbara.

Travel Route: Los Angeles to Santa Barbara via Malibu (100 miles)
Begin at La Brea Tar Pits, Wilshire Boulevard at Curson (near Fairfax). Continue west on Wilshire to Rodeo Drive. Park in this area and explore Beverly Hills. Then take Rodeo Drive north to Sunset Boulevard. Turn left (west) to Will Rogers State Historic Park in Pacific Palisades at 14235 Sunset Boulevard. Next take Sunset west to Highway 1 and head right (north) to the J. Paul Getty Museum. Continue north on Highway 1 (it merges with U.S. 101 in Oxnard) to Santa Barbara.

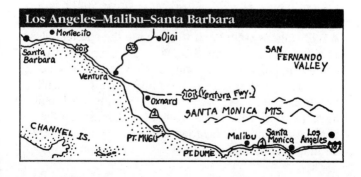

Los Angeles–Malibu–Santa Barbara

Sightseeing Highlights

▲▲La Brea Tar Pits—Located next door to the Los Angeles County Museum of Art, this is one of the richest fossil beds in America. More than 400 species of mammals, birds, reptiles, and fish have been uncovered here, and volunteers are still working with paleontologists in the excavation of Pit 91. The pits, found in Hancock Park, were pools of sticky asphalt. After seeing one of these tarry areas, walk on to the adjacent George C. Page Museum at 5801 Wilshire Boulevard, where you'll find reconstructed skeletons of extinct mammoths, mastodons, saber-toothed cats, and giant birds. Explore the park area first, then visit the museum, which is open from 10:00 a.m. to 5:00 p.m. Tuesday through Sunday. Closed Mondays, New Year's Day, Christmas, and Thanksgiving. Admission is $5 for adults, $1 for children. (213) 936-2330.

▲Beverly Hills—Rodeo Drive off Wilshire is the place to shop and browse. You'll find numerous boutiques offering fine designer clothes (Giorgio, Ted Lapidus), leather (Bottega Veneta), eyeglasses (Optica), and custom jewelry (Kenneth Jay Lane). One of the city's best delis, Nate 'n Al at 414 North Beverly Drive, is popular with celebrities. On my last visit I heard million-dollar deals discussed over bagels and lox. The Regent Beverly Wilshire at 9641 Sunset Boulevard and the Bel Air Hotel at 701 Stone Canyon Drive are two celebrity favorites worth a look. To extend your visit here, drive north along Cañon Drive and Benedict Canyon to Mulholland Drive for an over-view of the city. The Beverly Hills Visitors Bureau at 239 South Beverly Drive, 90212, is a good resource. Call (800) 345-2210 or (310) 271-8174.

▲Will Rogers State Park—Located in the coastal hills at 14253 Sunset Boulevard, this 186-acre state park encompasses the humorist's 18-room home, a stable, corrals, golf course, and polo field. It's a fine place for a picnic or a hike. If you take the tour, you'll see the ranch buildings, the room where Will wrote his columns, and the bronze sculptures by his friend Charles Russell. A popular trail offering fine marine views is the Inspiration Point

Loop. Admission is $3 per car; seniors, $2 per car.
(213) 454-8212.

▲▲▲**J. Paul Getty Museum**—This museum in the
Malibu hills fits perfectly in southern California's
Mediterranean climate, where lime trees dot the balmy
hills and surfers below paddle about on their boards,
waiting patiently for the perfect wave. The building is a
re-creation of the Villa dei Papiri, buried at Herculaneum
in the Mount Vesuvius eruption of A.D. The site of the
original villa was rediscovered by Italian treasure hunters
in the eighteenth century. While they searched for art,
archaeologists explored the tunnels and drew floor plans.
These documents provided the basis for the design of
Getty's museum, completed in 1974. With its peristyle
garden, colonnaded porticoes, pools, atrium, temple,
herb garden, and *cubicula* (bedrooms), this Malibu villa
re-creates the life-style of a prosperous Roman family.
The collection here, which embraces original Greek
sculptures, such as *The Victorious Athlete,* and a Cycladic
marble harpist from the Aegean Bronze Age, certainly
demonstrates what can be done with a budget of more
than $100 million a year. (Unless the museum spends this
sum, it faces adverse tax consequences.) But the success
of the Getty reflects more than its largesse: one of the
most extraordinary aspects of the museum is the way it
presents a major collection within the intimate villa setting; although the artworks are magnificent, there is nothing massive about the museum—in fact, many of its
finest pieces are miniatures, statuettes, and jewelry
housed in small alcoves.

   Particularly impressive are the terra-cotta statues of
Eros and Psyche, and a tiny Greek band of silver decorated with complex mythological scenes. Although some of
the museum's finest works—such as Titian's *Death of
Actaeon* or Van Dyck's *Portrait of Agostino Pallavicini*—
demonstrate what money can buy, this is not just the art
world's version of *Brewster's Millions.* Some of the most
pleasurable moments for any visitor are spent in lesser-
known parts of the museum. For instance, the decorative
arts collection provides a fine cross section of French,

Asian, and German craftsmanship. Small gems like the gilded soft-paste porcelain basket with green ground color are not to be missed. Also here are rarities like Madame de Pompadour's rococo vases with chinoiserie scenes. The pink, green, and dark blue coloring is the result of three firings on delicate porcelain.

Although he never lived to see the re-creation of Villa dei Papiri, John Paul Getty's vision has been realized. I can't think of a better place in America to sample Roman life or to view what billionaires like to collect in their spare time. The Getty Museum is open Tuesday through Sunday 10:00 a.m. to 5:00 p.m. Admission is free, but advance parking reservations are required. Call (310) 458-2003. If you can't get a reservation, the staff will explain where you can park nearby and catch a bus or taxi to the museum. Walk-in traffic is not permitted, but visitors without parking reservations may be dropped off at the front guardhouse or may arrive by bike, motorcycle, taxi, or RTD bus #434. Request a museum pass from the driver. For bus information, call (310) 458-2003.

Lodging
In Santa Barbara, the **Miramar Hotel-Resort**, at 1555 South Jameson Lane in Montecito, is located off U.S. 101. This 15-acre resort offers rooms for $75 to $145 on the beach. (805) 969-2203 or (800) 322-6983. Nearby is the **Four Seasons Biltmore**, at 1260 Channel Drive, 93108, a deluxe oceanfront establishment on 21 acres, with rooms starting at $299. (805) 969-2261. **Casa del Mar**, 18 Bath Street, 93101, offers rooms beginning at $70. (805) 963-4418. B&B rooms in the **Glenborough Inn** at 1327 Bath Street, 93101, run $70 to $165. Call (805) 966-0589. **Accommodations in Santa Barbara** is a central reservation service, (805) 687-9121. For visitor information, call the Santa Barbara Conference and Visitors Bureau at (805) 966-9222. The address is 510 State Street, Santa Barbara 93101. The local Chamber of Commerce, (805) 965-3023, can answer questions regarding individual travel plans.

Campers will want to try **Carpenteria State Beach**, 12 miles south of Santa Barbara on U.S. 101. Sites cost $14. Reserve ahead by calling (800) 444-7275. Another possibility for RVs is **Santa Barbara Sunrise RV Park** at 516 South Salinas. Units start at $20. Call (805) 966-9954.

Food

Many local residents, including Julia Child, like the Mexican food at **La Super-Rica**, 622 North Milpas, (805) 963-4940. Inexpensive. For Mexican seafood, try another inexpensive restaurant, **Pescados**, at 422 North Milpas, (805) 965-3805. The moderately priced **Wine Cask** at 813 Anacapa Street is a wine store that also has a fine bistro in the back offering pasta, chicken, and fish. Moderate. (805) 966-9463. For breakfast try **Fichera's Tree House** at 3860 State Street, (805) 687-2426. For Cajun, Creole, and Caribbean fare, head to the **Palace Café** at 8 East Cota Street. (805) 966-3133.

Optional Extension: Malibu

Casa Malibu at 22752 Pacific Coast Highway, (310) 456-2219, is a rare find. This is one of just three lodgings in the entire Los Angeles area right on the beach (not across the street). Rooms from $80 to $150 make this a good choice. If it's full, try the **Malibu Surfer** at 22541 Pacific Coast Highway. (310) 456-6169. Rooms range from $69 to $99. There's also camping at **Point Mugu State Park** north of Malibu. Reserve by calling (800) 444-7275. For park information, call (805) 987-3303. The Mexican food is popular at **Carlos and Pepe's**, 22706 Pacific Coast Highway, (310) 456-3105. Moderate. The **Sandcastle** at 28128 Pacific Coast Highway offers seafood dinners in the $10 to $25 range. It's on Paradise Cove, a private beach. (310) 457-2503. For budget–priced fish and chips, head to **Malibu Fish & SeaFood**, 25653 Pacific Coast Highway, (310) 456-3430.

In the Malibu area the best surfing is found at Surf Riders State Beach (part of Malibu Lagoon State Beach) and Zuma Beach in the 3000 block of Pacific Coast Highway. Doonesbury fans may want to reach the beach via the

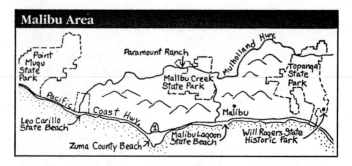

Zonker Harris Accessway at 22548 Pacific Coast Highway;
it's named for the tanning zealot. There are no changing
facilities at this point. Just north of Zuma, three pocket
beaches—El Matador, El Pescador, and La Piedra—offer
more protected cove swimming. Sycamore Cove, at 9000
Pacific Coast Highway in Point Mugu State Park, is
another good pocket beach popular for swimming and
fishing. After you're done at the beach, consider heading
inland to the old Paramount Ranch, now part of the
Santa Monica Mountains National Recreation Area. It's
reached off Highway 1 via Malibu Canyon Road and
Mulholland Drive. One hike here leads to the former
M*A*S*H set. (805) 888-3770.

Optional Extension: Ojai

There's a 24-hour outdoor bookstore, an apartment
house that resembles the Taj Mahal, and a private school
where every student gets his or her own horse. Film-
maker Frank Capra was so impressed by the view that he
used the snow-capped Topa Topa mountains here as the
setting for Shangri-La in his 1937 film, *Lost Horizon*. The
town is Ojai, pronounced "Oh Hi," just 15 miles off our
itinerary and 14 miles from the Ventura coast; it can be
easily reached by taking route 33 north from U.S. 101 in
Ventura. This region was originally home to the Chumash
Indians. It was later ruled by the Spanish and the
Mexicans who sold Rancho Ojai to a soldier named
Fernando Tico for $7,500. The town site was laid out in
1873 and soon became the subject of glowing reports by
Washington Post correspondent and author Charles

Nordhoff, who wrote of an idyllic valley carpeted with wildflowers and dominated by orange groves. Grateful for the tourism business generated by this Eastern writer, townspeople changed the community's name to Nordhoff until 1917 when it was renamed Ojai.

In the early 1920s, midwestern glass tycoon Edward Drummond Libbey became patron of this community. The glass magnate was so eager to turn Ojai's little shopping district into a Spanish arcade that he financed much of the expense out of his own pocket. The industrialist also created a new park and a handsome residential district called the Arbolada. In addition, he hired architect Wallace Neff to build an adobe-style hacienda called the Ojai Valley Inn. This popular retreat was later complemented by other resorts (many of which feature golf), inns, and spas. Today Ojai's principal enterprises are agriculture, tourism, motivational tapes, spas, and education.

A slow growth town that intends to hand out only about half a dozen building permits a year, Ojai "forces" its 7,500 residents to live without brand-name fast food. But there is no shortage of opportunities for spiritual growth in this community that was a power spot during the harmonic convergence. Visitors can study theosophy at the J. Krishnamurti Foundation or join the monthly full moon services on meditation mount.

On foot or by bike or car, it's easy to explore Ojai. You may want to see the Taj Mahal-like apartment building on Avenida de la Vereda, the famous Beatrice Wood pottery studio at 8560 Highway 150, and the Ojai Valley Museum on South Montgomery Street. One of the best vantage points in town is the Ojai Valley Inn's golf course which doubles as a country club. Be sure to explore the grounds here. Art and architecture tours offer a look at some of the Navajo Indian blankets, serigraphs, tapestries, watercolors, and classical pottery that grace the inn. Even after major renovations, much of the property remains just the way Neff designed it for Ojai patron Libbey. An attempt to connect two older buildings by cutting down an old oak tree was blocked by Ojai's tree preservation ordinance. The city fathers set a price tag of

$1 million for the permit necessary to take out the oak. As you might expect, the tree survives and the two buildings remain independent of one another. In this protectionist environment, is it any wonder that the Ojai of yesterday, today, and tomorrow are essentially one and the same?

For those who want to explore some of the region's backcountry there are many popular hiking trails. They range from a half-mile trip along Wheeler Gorge to a 10-mile trip along Mountain Ridge. An excellent choice is the hike up Matilija Canyon to Matilija Lake. You may spot fox, raccoon, deer, or bobcat along this oak-shaded path.

The U.S. Forest Service at 1190 East Ojai Avenue can also provide trail maps on the hundreds of miles of hiking trails open to backpackers in the Los Padres National Forest. Among the more than 140 miles of streams here is the Sespe River. If you prefer to explore by car, take the 11-mile Creek Road trip that begins at the south end of Ojai's Ventura Street and winds up in Oak View. A two-hour trip north of town via Highway 33 leads to Rose Valley where you can visit lakes, a spring, a waterfall, and Sespe Creek.

A highlight of any visit to Ojai is a stop at Bart's Books at Canada and Matilija streets. (805) 646-3755. Books are spread out across several cottages and a big courtyard complete with old oak trees. Entire sections are devoted to subjects ranging from Watergate to self-help. Cookbooks are found in the pantry of a former kitchen. You'll be helped by an engaging staff that includes one clerk who was married in the fiction section. It's not unusual to find readers pulling up to Bart's late at night and training their headlights on the shelves of used books mounted on the store's exterior walls. This store operates on the honor system with customers helping themselves to John Le Carré or Dick Francis and simply leaving money in the mail slot. I also recommend stopping by Vivika and Otto Pottery at 971 McAndrew Road, 3 miles east of town. Their work is great, and so is their tour.

A popular dining spot in a garden setting is the Ranch House, ten minutes fom Ojai on South Lomita, (805) 646-2360. Sea Fresh Seafood at 533 East Ojai Avenue, (805) 646-7747, offers patio dining. Ojai Ice Cream at 210 East Ojai Avenue has a great lemon sherbet.

In addition to the Ojai Valley Inn on Country Club Road, (805) 646-5511, which offers rooms at $195 and up, you can also stay at the Theodore Woolsey House bed and breakfast, 1484 East Ojai Avenue, where rooms run $55 to $110, (805) 646-9779. The Ojai Manor Hotel at 210 East Matilija Street offers bed and breakfast for $90 and up. (805) 646-0961.

SANTA BARBARA

John and Jackie Kennedy honeymooned here. That Richard Rodgers tune about a small hotel by a wishing well was written about a local inn. Celebrities from Jean Harlow to Gene Hackman have called this region home. And the American TV daytime soap opera named after this town was so hot in France they moved it to prime time. Today you'll have a chance to see some of the fine museums, parks, mansions, beaches, and historical sites. About the only thing you're likely to run out of along the way are favorable adjectives.

Suggested Schedule

9:00 a.m.	Santa Barbara Courthouse.
10:00 a.m.	Mission Santa Barbara.
11:00 a.m.	Museum of Natural History.
12:00 noon	Lunch at Rocky Nook County Park.
12:30 p.m.	Drive through Montecito.
1:30 p.m.	Red Tile Tour of historic Santa Barbara museums and adobes.
3:00 p.m.	The beach, more museums, shopping.

Santa Barbara
While this town may be considered a small one by California standards, there is nothing modest about Santa Barbara. Founded in 1782 as a Spanish presidio, the city later became a health resort. A model of intelligent community planning, this city of 85,000 demonstrates how tight zoning can create happiness. In downtown Santa Barbara, old Moorish-style theaters stand taller than office buildings, parking lots are paneled with wood, and sign ordinances enhance the neighborhood. Designed as a "home for those who seek refuge from the commonplace," Santa Barbara is enhanced by its Spanish architecture: even filling stations have tile roofs.

Visitors quickly find this is a great city for walking or riding a bike. With its beautiful gardens, Santa Ynez

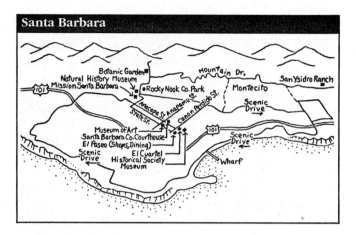

Santa Barbara

Botanic Garden
Natural History Museum
Mission Santa Barbara
101
Rocky Nook Co. Park
Mountain Dr.
San Ysidro Ranch
Montecito
Scenic Drive
Anacapa St. Anapamu St.
State St.
Canon Perdido St.
Museum of Art
Santa Barbara Co. Courthouse
El Paseo (Shops, Dining)
Scenic Drive
El Cuartel
Historical Society Museum
101
Scenic Drive
Wharf

mountain backdrop, and outdoor restaurants, Santa
Barbara adds definition to the California dream. Like
Pasadena and Berkeley, this city has done a fine job preserving many of its architectural landmarks. From the
mansions of Montecito to the mission-style homes near
downtown, this is the kind of place that instantly makes
Californians out of some visitors.

Sightseeing Highlights
▲▲▲**Santa Barbara County Courthouse**—Located
downtown on the 1100 block of Anacapa Street, this is
one of the finest public buildings in the American West.
Take the guided tour or, if you prefer, pick up a pam-
phlet and continue on your own for a look at this blend
of Mediterranean, Spanish, and Moorish design. One
highlight is the mural room where Daniel Groesbeck
gives us the history of California from Cabrillo's landing
in 1542 to General Fremont's arrival in Santa Barbara
three centuries later. Everything about this building is
oversized—from the vast, 21-foot wooden doors to the
clock tower cupola with its commanding view of the
ocean and the Santa Ynez Mountains. Although this is
a working courthouse, the museum quality is evident
in nearly every room. For instance, in the law library,
researchers work at antique walnut desks beneath
Gothic ceilings. There is also a museum hall with the

old presidio bell and Indian exhibits. Like many of Santa
Barbara's landmarks, the courthouse is surrounded by an
inviting park. In this case, the landscape is enhanced by
specimen trees from all over the state. (805) 962-6464.

▲**Mission Santa Barbara**—Go east two blocks from the
courthouse and turn left on Santa Barbara Street, continue to Mission Street and turn right to Mission Canyon
Road. Founded in 1786, this mission was rebuilt after the
1925 earthquake. A museum hall orients visitors, who
learn about the Chumash Indians and the Franciscan
fathers and see the mission's kitchen and adjacent grave-
yard. More than 4,000 Indians were buried at this site,
which is also the resting place of a number of local pioneer families. In use today as a parish church, this mission offers fine views of the city. An excellent time to
visit here is Old Spanish Days Fiesta in August. Every
Sunday before Christmas, a small Las Posadas pageant is
staged featuring dancing, singing, and breaking of the
piñata. Open 9:00 a.m. to 5:00 p.m. (805) 682-4149.

▲▲**Museum of Natural History**—Two blocks north of
the mission on Puesta del Sol Road, this museum is a
good place to learn about plate tectonics and to study
local geology and marine life. Inside the white stucco
buildings are good exhibits on mammals, birds, fish,
reptiles, and the Channel Islands. There's also a dio-
rama on Chumash Indian life. Children will be particularly interested in the mammal hall, observatory, and 72-
foot blue whale skeleton. Besides the extensive exhibits
here, it's possible to go on coastal tide pool walks or
whale-watching trips at appropriate times of the year.
Open 9:00 a.m. to 5:00 p.m. Monday through Saturday,
10:00 a.m. to 5:00 p.m. Sundays. Closed Thanksgiving,
Christmas, and New Year's. (805) 682-4711. The museum
is adjacent to your picnic spot, Rocky Nook County Park.

▲▲**Montecito Drive**—Take Alameda Padre Serra east
and veer right on Alston Road into Montecito. Follow the
blue Scenic Drive signs along Alston Road to Hot Springs
Road, and then turn south on Olive Mill Road to Channel
Drive. Along the way you'll find legendary resorts like
the San Ysidro Ranch, Marriott's Santa Barbara Biltmore,

and the Montecito Inn. Predictably, the spreads here have names such as El Eliseo, Ravenscroft, and Lotusland. There are grand colonial mansions, Mediterranean villas, Andalusian estates, and adobe-style ranch houses valued into the millions. Also here are plenty of upscale shopping opportunities. After stopping at the oceanfront Biltmore on Channel Drive, follow the Scenic Drive signs back to downtown. Stop at the Visitor Information Center at the corner of Cabrillo Boulevard and Santa Barbara Street to pick up the Red Tile Tour map, a 12-block walking tour through historic Santa Barbara.

▲▲**Arlington Theater**—Located in the 1300 block of State Street (between Victoria and Sola streets), on the site of a grand hotel damaged in the 1925 earthquake, this Moorish-style landmark is now a concert hall. The colonnaded arcade leads to this building inlaid with thirteenth-century Tunisian tiles, illuminated by chandeliers, and crowned by a landmark tower. Watching a performance here makes you feel like you're in Spain.

▲▲**Presidio**—Walk south on State Street and pick up the Red Tile route to Presidio Historic Park on East Cañon Perdido between Anacapa and Santa Barbara streets. The city was founded on this site in 1782. The Presidio, built by the Spanish, was one of four garrisons that protected their interests in Alta California. It served as both a military and government headquarters for this central California region. Here you can see the Canedo Adobe that once housed Presidio soldiers and their families, the Padres quarters, and the reconstructed chapel. Also here is El Cuartel, once adobe housing for soldiers and families, now a museum and gift shop. A local foundation hopes to restore the entire Presidio quadrangle as it looked in the late eighteenth century. El Cuartel is open weekdays from 10:30 a.m. to 4:30 p.m. and Saturdays and Sundays from noon to 4:00 p.m. (805) 966-9719.

▲**Historical Society Museum**—This tile-roofed adobe brick building at 136 East De la Guerra Street (also on the Red Tile route) explores the region's Indian, Spanish,

Mexican, and American periods. Showcased in the
Spanish room are pictures and manuscripts from the
Presidio and Mission periods. Also here is the bronze bell
donated to the Presidio Chapel by King Carlos III of
Spain in 1782. The adjacent Carrillo room is dedicated to
the city's founding fathers—mostly Mexicans who married Native Americans or blacks. The early American
period is explored in the Western Room. On display here
is the saddle of famed bandit Salomon Pico, who was the
inspiration for that well-known screen star, Zorro. Be
sure not to miss the museum's gold-leaf Chinese shrine
ornamented with dragons and phoenixes. Out on the
patio are an old gold stamp mill, antique choir stalls from
the old mission, and a two-ton anchor recovered from a
1915 shipwreck in the nearby Channel Islands. Open
Tuesday to Saturday 10:00 a.m. to 5:00 p.m. and Sunday
noon to 5:00 p.m. (805) 966-1601.

Itinerary Option
The Santa Barbara Botanic Garden at 1212 Mission
Canyon Road, 1.5 miles north of the mission, offers 5
miles of fine nature trails through 60 acres of indigenous
trees, shrubs, plants, and flowers. A must in the springtime. Open daily 8:00 a.m. to sunset. (805) 563-2521.

SAN SIMEON

After seeing the highlights of southern California, you are now entering one of the state's most scenic regions, the uncrowded central coast. With the Santa Ynez Mountains on one side and the Santa Barbara Channel on the other, this drive is a delight in any season. The spring wildflowers here are unforgettable. You will be tempted to stop at uncrowded beach parks like Refugio, a good vantage point for the Channel Islands. The inspiration for Scott O'Dell's classic novel for young people, *Island of the Blue Dolphins*, these islands are just one of many unspoiled central California landscapes. As you make the transition from urban California to the coastal wilderness, you'll pass through picturesque villages where high tea is served in the British tradition. You'll have a chance to explore tide pools and pause at Victorian inns dominated by gables and gingerbread. From the vast flowerbeds of Lompoc to the wineries of San Luis Obispo County, you'll find this area ideal for leisurely countryside drives and strolls. Of course, the highlight of your relaxed drive up the coast will be a visit to William Randolph Hearst's fabled Xanadu, San Simeon.

Suggested Schedule

8:00 a.m.	Breakfast.
9:00 a.m.	Head north along the coast on U.S. 101.
10:00 a.m.	Pause for pastry in Solvang.
12:00 noon	Lunch in Cayucos at Bill and Carol's Sea Shanty, an old-time diner.
2:00 p.m.	Begin Tour #1 at San Simeon.
5:00 p.m.	Swim at your motel.
6:00 p.m.	Dinner, followed by a leisurely stroll through the village of San Simeon. Walk along the beach at sunset.

The Central Coast

Before checking out of your beach motel in Santa Barbara, be sure you have confirmed reservations for today's trip to San Simeon. Details are found in Helpful Hints at the end of Day 7. Return to U.S. 101 and turn left (north) for the drive up the coast. After crossing Gaviota Pass, you'll come to Buellton, where you turn right (east) on S.R. 246 for the 4-mile trip to Solvang. This half-timbered Danish fantasy town is a perfect place for a pastry and a stroll. Many celebrities, including Ronald and Nancy Reagan, have homes here in or near the Santa Ynez Valley. Returning on S.R. 246 west to U.S. 101, you'll turn right (north) and make the hour-long drive to your next stop, at San Luis Obispo's Madonna Inn. Here, room decor ranges from rococo to early Flintstone, the garage features stained-glass windows, and bathrooms are equipped with waterfalls. Return to U.S. 101 south and take the S.R. 1 exit north to the coast. Continue through Morro Bay, distinguished by its towering landmark, Morro Rock. An ideal side trip, the state park here is understandably popular with RVers, campers, swimmers, hikers, and bird-watchers.

S.R. 1 becomes a two-lane highway as you begin the 100-mile journey along California's Big Sur coast. Big-city life is replaced by a handful of small towns like Cambria, where you'll check into your motel.

Lodging

San Simeon, Cambria, and Cayucos offer more than two dozen lodging alternatives ranging from romantic oceanfront inns to charming small town bed and breakfasts. Just 12 miles south of the castle and close to a number of good restaurants, Cambria is the logical place to stay. This artists' colony of 4,000 is perhaps best known for Nitwit Ridge, an eclectic hillside home that has been under construction since 1928. Owner Art Beal has used beer bottles, bicycle parts, and thousands of other odds and ends to get the job done.

On the way uup to San Simeon, I highly recommend **Garden Street Inn** at 1212 Garden Street in San Luis Obispo. This $90- to $160-a-night Bed and Breakfast is

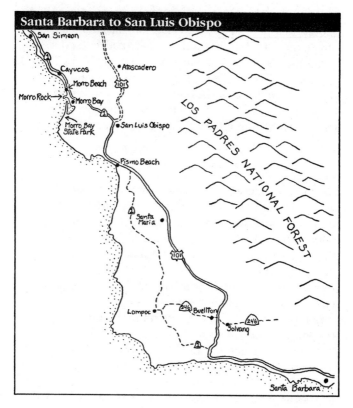

Santa Barbara to San Luis Obispo

one of the region's winners. Ask to see the *Field of Dreams* baseball memorabilia room. (805) 545-9802

Our deluxe choice in Cambria is the ranch-style **San Simeon Pines Resort Motel**, adjacent to S.R. 1 at Santa Barbara to San Luis Obispo Moonstone Beach Drive, (805) 927-4648. There's a direct path to Leffingwell Landing, where you may spot sea lions, sea otters, or migrating whales. Bring your golf clubs and you can try the free par 3 (nine-hole) golf course. Rates are $68 to $90.

The **Victorian Pickford House** is a good bed and breakfast alternative at 2555 MacLeod Avenue, (805) 927-8619. In addition to a full breakfast, you can enjoy cheese and crackers, beer, and wine each afternoon in the nineteenth-century pub. The eight rooms run from about $85 for a single to $125 for a double.

A good budget accommodation here is the **Blue Bird Motel**. In a pine-shaded garden setting at 1880 Main Street, the Blue Bird is a welcome alternative to cookie-cutter motels. Rooms start around $40. Call (805) 927-4634.

The most convenient place for RVs and campers is **San Simeon State Park** on the ocean, 4 miles north. Showers are available here. Reserve a site by calling (800) 444-7275 in California or (619) 452-1950 out of state.

Food

As you'd expect in a California town with a British flavor, Cambria has several promising restaurants. For supper, try **Brambles Dinner House**, a handsome English cottage built in 1874. This antique-filled establishment is the place for prime rib or fresh salmon. It's located at 4005 Burton Drive, and reservations are recommended. (805) 927-4716. The **Sow's Ear**, 2248 Main Street, specializes in moderate to expensive steaks, seafood, and pasta. (805) 927-4865. On a warm night, dine outside at the **Hamlet Restaurant** at Moonstone Gardens. It's located 1.5 miles north of Cambria on S.R. 1 across from Moonstone Beach. Reservations are recommended. (805) 927-3535. While you can buy sandwiches and snacks at San Simeon, consider picnicking at the park instead. The century-old **San Simeon Store** is a convenient place to buy supplies as well as books on the castle and reasonably priced souvenirs. Be sure to browse in this eclectic establishment located across the street from a warehouse that is crammed with part of Hearst's art collection.

San Simeon

William Randolph Hearst's "ranch," San Simeon is divided into four tours. Begin with Tour #1, which gives you an overview of this 165-room estate. Begun in 1919, the project was under construction for 28 years and remained unfinished at the time of Hearst's death in 1951. Due to the $6,000-a-day expense of operating this mansion, the Hearst estate was unable to sell it at any price. Even Frank Sinatra took a pass. The State of California reluctantly agreed to take over the white elephant in 1957, and today San Simeon is one of the most successful units in the park system.

Modeled after a Spanish cathedral, the castle brings together baroque, medieval, Renaissance, Moorish, and Florentine treasures collected by the publisher. You may see some of the zebra and Barbary sheep that were part of his private zoo. On Tour #1, you'll take a walk through the garden and see what is arguably the handsomest plunge in America, the Neptune Pool. Inside the castle you'll find such treasures as the refectory with its polished silver and Flemish tapestries and the baroque Assembly Room. It was here that Hearst emerged from an elevator hidden behind the choir stalls and greeted his guests each evening. If you're eager for more at the end of Tour #1, buy a ticket for Tour #2 where you'll see Hearst's private Gothic Suite, the Della Robbia room featuring Italian Renaissance terra-cotta sculptures, and the paneled library. Tour #3 provides a look at one of three guest houses and the mansion's north wing, giving you a chance to compare Morgan's 1920s architectural and decorative techniques with those of the late 1940s. A highlight of this visit is a film of Hearst's celebrity guests in the 1920s and 1930s, including many in masquerade costume. Evening tours are offered in the spring and fall. They take the visitor back in time to the castle's heyday in the 1930s with the help of Living History Docents, who stroll the grounds portraying Mr. Hearst's "guests" and "domestic staff."

Helpful Hints

Remember that you must buy your San Simeon tickets before arriving. To make reservations, call (800) 444-7275. Tours leave at least once every hour from 8:20 a.m. to 3:00 p.m. in the winter and more frequently during the holidays and the summer season. The book to read before you come is *Citizen Hearst* by W. A. Swanberg. And by all means, if you haven't seen it lately, check out a video of *Citizen Kane* before beginning your trip.

DAY 8
BIG SUR

After leaving the splendor of San Simeon, Highway 1 doesn't hit another town of consequence for nearly 100 miles. Built largely by convict labor across a cliffside landscape subject to slides and washouts, this road is certainly not for the faint of heart. To enjoy it, just throttle down and take your time on this, the main line to Big Sur. Conceived by optimists in 1920 and completed fourteen years later with the help of some of San Quentin's road gangs, this is probably the finest stretch of highway on the West Coast.

Suggested Schedule

8:00 a.m.	Leave San Simeon on Highway 1 north.
9:00 a.m.	Explore southern Big Sur coast.
11:00 a.m.	Visit Julia Pfeiffer Burns State Park.
12:00 noon	Visit Henry Miller Library.
12:30 p.m.	Lunch at Pfeiffer Big Sur State Park.
2:00 p.m.	Visit Pfeiffer Beach, then check in at Big Sur or continue north toward Carmel.
4:00 p.m.	Visit Point Lobos.
5:30 p.m.	Arrive Carmel/Monterey.

Travel Route: San Simeon to Monterey (96 miles)

Take Highway 1 north, stopping to walk along the coast at either Jade Cove (32 miles north) or Kirk Creek Campground (36 miles north). Continue 18 miles to Julia Pfeiffer Burns State Park. Five miles north on the right side of the road is the Henry Miller Library. Continue 6 miles north to Pfeiffer Big Sur State Park. Leaving the park, turn south (left) on Highway 1 for one mile to Sycamore Canyon Road, and turn right on Sycamore Canyon Road to Pfeiffer Beach. Spend the night in the Big Sur area, or continue north 24 miles on Highway 1 to Point Lobos and turn left into the reserve. Carmel is one mile north. Continue 3 more miles to Monterey.

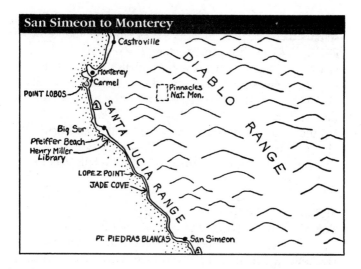

The Big Sur Coast

Flanked by the Santa Lucia Mountains, this coastal paradise was virtually inaccessible until the mid-nineteenth century when a handful of pioneers colonized the area to log its redwood and quarry its limestone. Although there was a rough road north to Salinas, the only way south was a difficult inland route over the Santa Lucias to Jolon and King City. Pioneers like John Roberts, a country doctor from Monterey, worked hard to convince the state legislature that all of California would benefit from the construction of a modern coastal highway linking Carmel with San Simeon. The job began in 1920 as crews made their way south from Piedras Blancas lighthouse, across Salmon Creek into Big Sur and Anderson Canyon. The project stalled, due to a change of political command in Sacramento; later it continued south, spanning a total of thirty-two streams and ravines with redwood trestles and concrete and steel bridges. At the time of its construction, one of the parabolic spans you'll cross today—the 550-foot-long, 260-foot-high Bixby Creek Bridge—was the largest of its type in the world. Completed at a cost of $10 million in 1934, the Cabrillo Highway is Big Sur's main line. Author Henry Miller, who lived and wrote here for eighteen years (see his *Big Sur and the Oranges* `of Hieronymus Bosch*), was convinced that as the early settlers died off, their "huge tracts of land" would be broken up into a suburb (of Monterey) "which has barbeque stands, gas stations, chain stores and all the other claptrap that makes suburbia horrendous." Miller was wrong. Today only about 1,000 people live in the Big Sur community, where tight zoning has saved the day. Even during the peak summer season, when traffic builds up along Highway 1, you are only minutes away from deserted trails, beaches, streams, and waterfalls. Get an early start.

Sightseeing Highlights

▲▲**Jade Cove**—Located three miles north of Gorda, Jade Cove can be reached by a steep path down from the highway. In 1971 the world's largest piece of jade (8.5 by 5 feet, weighing over 9,000 pounds) was found here. You can see this famous Pacific blue jade on Day 22 at the Oakland Museum courtyard garden. Although a Gorda firm has a permit to take and sell jade here, visitors are not allowed to remove any stone above the mean high-tide level. Unless you're a diver, you'll have to wait until the tide goes out for a chance to pick up jade or green serpentine. As at any coastal location, keep a close eye on the tides. Swimming is a mistake. Also, proceed cautiously on the precipitous trails. Children must be kept close at hand at all times and should be under adult supervision.

▲▲**Kirk Creek Campground**—Another steep trail leads down from this 100-foot-high coastal overlook. An excellent place for surf fishing, beachcombing, photography, kite flying, and seal and sea otter watching.

▲▲**Julia Pfeiffer Burns State Park**—At this 2,045-acre state park named for a pioneer Big Sur homesteader, you can hike down to an old Pelton water wheel, or hike beneath the Cabrillo Highway to a fine coastal overlook. Here you can also see the McWay Creek waterfall. The coastline is part of an underwater reserve. To reach it, hike down Partington Canyon through a tunnel to Partington Cove, an old lumber port. A more ambitious trip is a hike into the park's upper reaches along the Ewoldsen or Tan Bark Trail. Your hike here leads along the streambeds canopied by tan oaks, madrones, and California laurels. (408) 667-2316.

▲**Henry Miller Library**—"Miller was a big sponger," said his friend Emil White. The author's house here in paradise was a gift from a local woman. While he aspired to the simple life, Miller saw no reason to walk. "He bought a $100 Cadillac," White recalled shortly before his death in 1989, "but his friends had to spend thousands to help him keep it running." The author, who lived here on Big Sur's Partington Ridge from 1944 to 1962, did pay back some of his long-term debts when he struck a commercial literary vein in the 1960s. Ironically, part of that windfall came from his writing about Big Sur. In part, people paid to read his gloomy forecast of Big Sur's decline and fall. At this library, located in White's former home, guests can sample Miller's collected works, see his paintings, and read some of his letters, criticism, and articles. (408) 667-2574.

▲▲▲**Pfeiffer Beach**—Located at the end of Sycamore Canyon Road, this is the place to see the sun rise or set. In fact, it's a good place to visit just about any time. Imposing arches provide a romantic setting and make it one of the most popular beaches in the area.

▲▲**Pfeiffer Big Sur State Park**—With 80 miles of hiking trails, it's easy to get lost here for a few hours or a few days. Among the more popular trails is the trip through a redwood grove to Pfeiffer Falls. Ambitious types can make the strenuous 4.5-mile trip up 3,100-foot-high Mount Manuel. The park backs up on the Ventana Wilderness, a popular hiking and backpacking area that includes the Arroyo Seco, Carmel, and Little and Big Sur rivers. This backcountry haven, with hundreds of miles of trails, is part of the Los Padres National Forest District extending nearly all the way south to San Simeon. Whether you take the Pine Ridge Trail into the backcountry or simply go for an easy stroll through the fields of lupine, lilies, Indian paintbrush, and California poppies, you may find evidence of several recent natural calamities. They include two major fires as well as landslides. (408) 667-2315.

▲▲**Point Lobos**—One of the state's best wildlife sanctuaries. On the headlands, amid the increasingly rare Monterey cypress trees, you may be able to see whales and two species of sea lions and sea otters, or visit the underwater tide pool reserve. On this 1,276-acre reserve there are more than 300 plant species. No wonder it was a favorite resting place of poet Robinson Jeffers and the inspiration for Robert Louis Stevenson's Spyglass Hill in *Treasure Island*. Access is capacity controlled, and there's a $6 vehicle charge. If you don't want to wait to drive in on a busy weekend, park your car outside the entrance and walk in. (408) 624-4909.

Lodging

In the Big Sur area, the **Big Sur Lodge** at Pfeiffer Big Sur State Park is a central location offering cottages, some with kitchens, and a heated swimming pool, as well as a restaurant and small grocery store. Rooms run $89 to $179. (408) 667-2171. North of the park on Highway 1, is the **Ripplewood Resort** with housekeeping cabins in the redwoods, including some on the Big Sur River. Rates are $45 to $80. (408) 667-2242. South of the park on Highway 1 is **Deetjen's Big Sur Inn**. No two rooms are alike at this little piece of Norway tucked beneath the redwoods. Rates range from $66 to $136. The restaurant here is also popular for breakfast and dinner. (408) 667-2377. For total luxury and prices to match, **Ventana Inn** is a good choice. Rates start at $175 to $195, depending on the season. Children are not welcome. (408) 667-2331.

Campers: Campsites at **Pfeiffer Big Sur State Park** may be reserved by calling (800) 444-7275. Available on a first-come, first-served basis are campsites at **Andrew Molera State Park**, 4.7 miles north of Pfeiffer Big Sur. **Big Sur Campground and Cabins** at Highway 1, Big Sur 93920, also offers sites at $20. (408) 667-2322. **Riverside Campground and Cabins** has spaces for $22. (408) 667-2414. Write to Box 3, Big Sur 93920.

In the Carmel area, **Mission Ranch**, owned by Clint
Eastwood, has an enviable location overlooking a meadow
and the ocean. Cottages and B&B rooms in a historic
house, tennis courts, hiking trails, and access to the mission make this a popular choice. Rooms begin around
$85. Located at 26270 Dolores, 93923, (408) 624-6436. In
Carmel Valley, **Robles del Rio Lodge** at 200 Punta del
Monte, 93924, offers a mountaintop B&B setting with
rooms from $75 to $115. (408) 659-3705. If you prefer to
stay in the midst of a country club, complete with an 18-
hole golf course, consider **Quail Lodge** at 8205 Valley
Greens Drive, 93923. (408) 624-1581. Rooms start at
$225. Try the Covey Restaurant, expensive. Also recom-
mended is the exclusive **Carmel Valley Ranch Resort**,
1 Old Ranch Road. (408) 625-9500. Deluxe suites start
at $235. In Pacific Grove, the **Asilomar Conference
Grounds** at 800 Asilomar Boulevard, 93950, accepts
individuals. If space is available, you can reserve a room
at this lovely oceanfront state park unit up to one week
in advance. Rooms start around $60. Credit cards are not
accepted. (408) 372-8016. Monterey's **Victorian Inn** at
487 Foam Street, 93940, is convenient to Cannery Row
and the aquarium. Modern units with fireplaces adjoin
a handsome Victorian house where a complimentary
breakfast is served. Rooms start at $99. (408) 373-8000.
The deluxe **Monterey Plaza** at 400 Cannery Row, 93940,
offers bay views. Units begin at $150. (408) 646-1700.
Many moderately priced motels are also located here.
Borg's Motel at 635 Ocean View Boulevard, Pacific
Grove 93950, offers units beginning at $48. (408) 375-2406.
For home stay B&Bs, contact **B&B International**,
1181-B Solano Avenue, Albany 94706, or call (800)
872-4500. Rooms range from $65 to $150. Luxurious
oceanfront condominiums are also available 18 miles
north of Monterey at **Monterey Dunes**, Box 308, Moss
Landing 95039. Units start at $140 to $200, depending
on the season. (408) 633-4883. Another possibility a
few miles farther north is **Pajaro Dunes** at 2661 Beach
Road, Watsonville 95076. Condos begin at about $400,
with a two night minimum; (408) 722-9201. These places

are well situated if you plan to extend your visit to
Santa Cruz.

Monterey Peninsula Youth Hostel is located in one
or more local schools and provides mattresses on the
floor from June 11 to August 21. The charge is $8 per
person. (408) 298-0670. Contact the hostel c/o Monterey
YMCA, P.O. Box 1013, Monterey 93940.

Riverside RV Park at Route 2, Carmel 93923, offers
campsites for $30. It's located 4.5 miles east of town in
Carmel Valley on Schulte Road. (408) 624-9329.

Food
In the Carmel area, **Creme Carmel** at San Carlos Street
and Seventh Avenue serves fresh fish and beef. Expensive.
(408) 624-0444. For good inexpensive breakfasts, try
Katy's Place at Mission and Sixth Avenue. (408) 624-
0199. Or try the Japanese food at **Robata Grill and Sake
Bar**, 3658 The Barnyard, Carmel. (408) 624-2643. **Fresh
Cream** at 99 Pacific Street in Monterey serves expensive
French cuisine. (408) 375-9798. **Domenico's** at 50
Fisherman's Wharf is a popular, albeit expensive, place
for seafood and pasta. (408) 372-3655. A less expensive
place for seafood is **Abalonetti's** at #1 Fisherman's
Wharf; try the calamari. (408) 646-0351. Also serving
moderately priced fresh fish is the **Fishery** at 21 Soledad
Drive, (408) 373-6200. A good place for outdoor patio
dining is the **Clock Garden Restaurant** at 565 Abrego.
Continental food, fresh fish, moderate. (408) 375-6100. In
nearby Pacific Grove there's inexpensive Mexican food at
Pablo's, 1184 Forest Avenue. (408) 646-8888. If you're
driving north toward Santa Cruz, you might want to
detour to **Zuniga's**, a venerable Mexican restaurant
known for its tamales and chile rellenos. It's at the
Watsonville Airport, 100 Aviation Way, Watsonville.
(408) 724-5788. Inexpensive.

Helpful Hint
For more information on this region, contact the
Monterey Peninsula Chamber of Commerce at P.O.
Box 1770, Monterey 93940. (408) 649-1770.

CARMEL AND MONTEREY

The village of Carmel, Pebble Beach, the Monterey Bay Aquarium, Cannery Row, and the Monterey Path of History—these are some of today's highlights. Many people like to call this region "Steinbeck Country," but he is only one of several authors and poets—ranging from Robert Louis Stevenson to Robinson Jeffers—who wrote great literature here. You'll visit the mission where Father Junípero Serra was laid to rest and the town where drivers who make the mistake of not stopping after hitting a tree can wind up in jail. There'll be a chance to see kelp forests, large sharks, and sea otters. If you wish, pay for the privilege of seeing how the other half lives, or tee off on the golf courses that Bing Crosby made famous.

Suggested Schedule	
9:00 a.m.	Carmel Mission.
10:00 a.m.	Visit Carmel.
11:00 a.m.	17 Mile Drive.
12:00 noon	Lunch.
1:00 p.m.	Monterey Bay Aquarium/Cannery Row.
3:30 p.m.	Walking Tour of historic Monterey.
	Balance of afternoon at leisure.

Travel Route
Take Rio Road west off Highway 1 in Carmel to Carmel Mission. Continue north on Junipero Avenue to 13th Avenue and turn left. At Scenic Road, turn left again to the Carmel River State Beach. Return north on Scenic to Carmel Beach at the foot of Ocean Avenue. After visiting here, walk or drive up Ocean to downtown Carmel. Then drive north on San Antonio Avenue to Carmel Way. Follow this road to the beginning of the 17 Mile Drive through Pebble Beach. At the gatehouse, you'll pay $6.75 per car and receive a local map from a guard who can direct you. To take the complete circuit simply follow the 17 Mile Drive signs and exit at the Highway 1 gate.

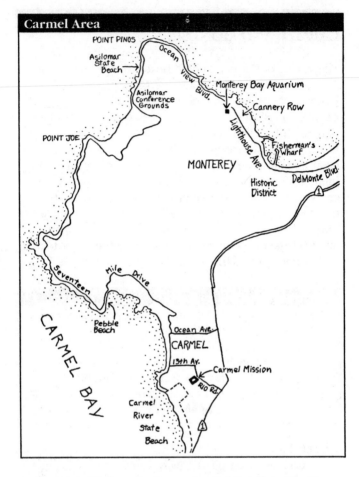

Follow S.R. 68 (Pacific Grove-Carmel Road) north. Turn
right on David Avenue, which leads to Cannery Row
and the Monterey Bay Aquarium. A more direct route
through Pebble Beach is to turn left when you enter
the 17 Mile gate from Carmel. Follow the road past the
Pebble Beach Golf Course and continue along the coast
to the Pacific Grove gate. Turn left on Sunset Drive and
loop around Point Pinos to Ocean View Boulevard. This
road becomes Lighthouse Avenue in Monterey. Turn left
on David Avenue to Cannery Row and the aquarium.
Continue east on Lighthouse Avenue to Pacific Street in

downtown Monterey. Park between Jefferson and Madison in the vicinity of Colton Hall.

Sightseeing Highlights

▲▲**Carmel Mission**—Here, graced by lilies of the Nile, agapanthus, Martha Washingtons, hydrangea, bougainvillea, and Mexican sage cactus, is California's storybook mission. It was one of nine California missions created by Father Junípero Serra, the Franciscan who brought Christianity to the Indians. Restored to its 1793 glory, this Moorish stone church is a showplace for silver altar furnishings, hand-embroidered pillow cases, and black Chinese lacquer boxes. You'll learn about the Indians who, like Father Serra, came to learn the meaning of poverty, obedience, and penance here. While the missions may not have succeeded in their goal of bettering the lot of the Native American community, they remain the inspiration for a major school of California architecture and provide a convenient marker for looking at the state's roots. They also outline some of the earliest European efforts to tame part of the Wild West. Many myths surround portions of this story, but there is no doubting the heroic role played by Father Serra, who died in a small cell here in 1874. Exhumed twice by the church, he has already been credited with one miracle healing, and he could become California's first saint. (408) 624-3600.

▲▲**Carmel**—Historian Kevin Starr notes that Carmel's founding fathers were a pragmatic lot: "Devoid of program or ideology, Carmel had shrewd foundations in real estate." Successful artists like George Sterling were even given low-interest real estate loans "to help attract the right clientele." But some famous visitors like Jack London were put off by the peculiar Carmelites who played out little "psychodramas against a backdrop of mental torment." Today it's hard to imagine what could ever go wrong in Carmel, aside from the difficulty of getting a room reservation on a weekend. Strolling down Ocean Avenue you'll find yourself in the midst of pleasant Tudor inns, Asian galleries, and Swedish bakeries offering baguettes fresh out of the oven. The July Bach Festival, with some events staged at the mission, is not to be missed. And how can you criticize a city that keeps computerized records of every single tree to make sure no one trims—let alone removes—a cypress or pine without government consent. With its fine white sand and cypress backdrop, Carmel Beach at the foot of Ocean Avenue looks like it was lifted from a very pleasant dream. For evening excitement, you might want to check out the **Hog's Breath Inn** on San Carlos Street at 5th Avenue. Partially owned by former Mayor Clint Eastwood, it's the place to enjoy a Dirty Harry Burger.

▲**17 Mile Drive**—For $6.00 you can drive through the Del Monte Forest and see the mansions of Pebble Beach and the golf courses that were once the site of the Bing Crosby Pro-Am. The crooner's widow refused to share joint billing with a corporate sponsor and the event lives on as the AT&T Pebble Beach Pro-Am. Besides enjoying the views, marine mammals, and birdlife, you may want to stop at the handsome Lodge at Pebble Beach, head-quarters for this PGA tournament.

▲▲▲**Monterey Bay Aquarium**—Not just the biggest, it's also probably the best aquarium in California, possibly even the United States. At $9.75 ($7.25 for students and seniors and $4.50 for children), tickets go fast; you may want to make reservations through Ticketron for weekends or holidays. Major exhibits include the third-of-a-million-gallon kelp forests that provide a diver's view of the deep; hidden jets keep the 66-foot-long, 28-foot-high forest in perpetual motion. This is also the ideal place to watch fun-loving sea otters. All of the sea otters living here were rescued and raised by the aquarium staff with volunteer help. Another big hit is the Monterey Bay exhibit, where large sharks, bat rays, salmon, striped bass, and many other fish have the run of a 90-foot-long exhibit (future plans call for adding a great white shark). Special viewing windows give visitors the big picture. Related exhibits include a slough, a coastal stream, and a walk-through aviary with shorebirds like snowy plovers, stilts, avocets, and killdeer. All children, and many parents, will want to pick up some of the bat rays in the bat ray petting pool. By the way, my favorite California museum pun is found at the display showing how marine trash becomes fish habitat: "One man's junk is anemone shelter." After visiting the aquarium, explore adjacent Cannery Row, a dolled-up version of the neighborhood Steinbeck immortalized. At one time this was a world-renowned sardine-packing capital. Then, in 1945, sardines disappeared from local waters. As a result all eighteen canneries have gone out of business, leaving the door open for all sorts of tourist-related enterprises. Today's Cannery Row has weak ties to the book of the same name. Even the building that formed the basis for Doc Rickett's laboratory has been turned into a private club. The aquarium is located at 886 Cannery Row. (408) 648-4888.

▲▲**Path of History**—Sixty years after Juan Rodriguez Cabrillo claimed California for Spain, Sebastian Vizcaino founded Monterey. Colonized in 1770 by Father Serra and Don Gaspar de Portola, this city attracted many seafarers from New England who adapted the Spanish colonial architecture into a new Monterey style. The Larkin House on Jefferson between Pacific and Calle Principal was the model for many of these early buildings; this two-story adobe with a hip roof, balcony, and veranda is furnished with many original Larkin pieces. It is just one of the landmarks on the 3-mile-long Path of History tour leading through the heart of this city that was the California capital under Spain, Mexico, and, for a brief period, the United States. Crossing Pacific you'll come to Colton Hall, the first public building of California's American period and site of the state's first constitutional convention. There are many other landmarks on this walk, such as California's First Theatre, Casa Gutierrez, and the Custom House. One of the most popular stops is the Stevenson House on Houston Street between Pearl and Webster; Robert Louis Stevenson lived in this boardinghouse in 1879 and divided his time between writing and trying to persuade Fanny Osbourne—a woman he had met in Europe—to leave her husband and marry him. He succeeded the following year. In this area you can also visit the Maritime Museum of Monterey at 5 Custom House Plaza. (408) 373-2469. Here you'll see intriguing displays on the region's seafaring past. Open Tuesday-Sunday 10:00 a.m. to 5:00 p.m. Admission $5 adults, $2 children 6 to 12. Under 5 free.

Itinerary Option: Steinbeck's Home, Salinas

Just 17 miles east of Monterey via S.R. 68 is Salinas, the birthplace of John Steinbeck. The heart of a major farming region, the Salinas area is the setting for some of his finest work. Breaking in as a reporter on his high school paper, *El Gabilan*, Steinbeck went on to Stanford University and also worked with the migrant farmers and the ranchers of his native Salinas Valley. His birthplace, at 132 Central, offers lunch in the tearoom Monday through Friday. You need to make reservations a week in advance. (408) 424-2735. This landmark is in the midst of a historic downtown district graced with handsomely restored Victorians and Gothic revivals. From the Steinbeck house, continue east to Church Street and then turn right to San Luis. Turn left here to Pajaro and you'll come to the Presbyterian Church that was part of the story line in *East of Eden*. Today it's a restaurant called, you guessed it, East of Eden. Also of interest here is the John Steinbeck Library, at 110 West San Luis, where the author did considerable research. In the Steinbeck room are photos, first editions, original manuscripts, and other memorabilia. Steinbeck's grave is at Garden of Memories, 768 Abbott.

Itinerary Option: Santa Cruz

Located 29 miles north of Monterey via Highway 1, this city is northern California's favorite beach resort and home of a University of California campus pretty enough to make anyone want to be a student. The main attraction in town is the Santa Cruz Beach Boardwalk, built in 1907. It was one of many amusement parks—such as San Francisco's Playland at the Beach and The Pike at Long Beach—that entertained Californians up and down the

coast. Today only the boardwalk remains. The landmark
here is the 64-year-old Giant Dipper. This ride, with its
70-foot drop and half-mile track, makes just about every
list of the world's top ten wooden roller coasters. More
than 25 million riders have climbed aboard, some only
once. Last of the old-fashioned amusement parks on the
West Coast, the Boardwalk offers many other rides and
ballroom dancing on weekends.

From the Boardwalk you can also catch a ride on the
historic Santa Cruz, Big Trees & Pacific Railway train up
into the redwoods at Roaring Camp. This 6-mile-long
excursion follows part of the old rail route that Bay Area
residents took to reach Santa Cruz on day trips. You can
stop along the way to enjoy the swimming pool at the
Garden of Eden. Other popular sites in Santa Cruz
include the Surfing Museum on West Cliff Drive at
Lighthouse Point (open noon to 5:00 p.m. Thursdays
through Sundays) and the Mystery Spot at 1953
Branciforte Road. Gravity doesn't seem to function here
as balls roll uphill and visitors have a hard time keeping
their balance. Great for kids! Information on these activi-
ties and numerous walking tours in the historic central
city is available from the Chamber of Commerce at 1543
Pacific Avenue, (408) 423-1111. Or visit the tourist information booth at 611 Ocean Street near the Holiday Inn.

SAN JUAN BAUTISTA TO YOSEMITE

Today a leisurely drive across the Salinas Valley takes you to the loveliest of the California mission towns, San Juan Bautista. From here you cut across the San Joaquin Valley to Yosemite National Park where there will be time to enjoy a relaxing stroll along the valley floor before dinner. Enjoy a nightcap at a castle hewn from stone and cedar.

Suggested Schedule

8:00 a.m.	Monterey to San Juan Bautista.
9:00 a.m.	Visit historic San Juan Bautista.
11:00 a.m.	Drive to Yosemite.
3:30 p.m.	Visit Yosemite Valley.
8:00 p.m.	Nightcap at the Ahwahnee Hotel.

Travel Route (242 miles)

Your trip begins with a 27-mile drive via Highway 1 north and S.R. 156 east to San Juan Bautista. After visiting here, you'll drive another 215 miles to Yosemite National Park. From San Juan Bautista, take S.R. 156 east to S.R. 152 over Pacheco Pass. Turn north on S.R. 59 at Red Top to Merced where you pick up S.R. 140 to Yosemite National Park's El Portal entrance. Continue to Yosemite Village where you can check into your lodge, cabin, or campground.

Alternate Route: Pacheco Pass is not recommended at night or in foggy or stormy weather. If you're in doubt, check with Caltrans at (916) 445-7623. An alternate route is U.S. 101 north from San Juan Bautista to Interstate 680 in San Jose. Continue north to Pleasanton and pick up Interstate 580 east to Tracy and Interstate 205. Continue east to Manteca. Begin Highway 120 east here to Yosemite's Big Oak Flat entrance on to Yosemite Valley.

San Juan Bautista

Often overlooked by travelers hurrying down U.S. 101, San Juan Bautista is cooled by the breezes blowing in

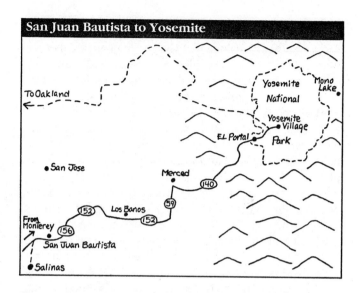

San Juan Bautista to Yosemite

from Monterey Bay across the Salinas Valley. This town
of 1,200 rests squarely on the San Andreas Fault.
Although that rift has torn the mission apart, its recon-
struction is one of El Camino Real's architectural master-
pieces. It is located on a beautiful plaza that includes a
pair of century-old mansions, a hotel, stables, a blacksmith shop, and a wash house. They are open daily 10:00
a.m. to 5:00 p.m. for an admission fee of $1 for adults
and 50 cents for children. This historic park is the corner-
stone of a community that seems to get better with each
passing year. Just pick up the walking tour brochure at
the park headquarters in the Castro Adobe on the plaza,
(408) 623-4881, or the Chamber of Commerce at Third
and Washington, (408) 623-2454, and you're ready to go.

The mission, once home to 1,200 Indians, is com-
posed of two wings. The rectangular church is complemented by a Moorish cloister and two adobe structures.
Particularly impressive is the sanctuary altar framed by a
large wooden structure called a *reredo*. Decorated with
paint made from vegetable and mineral dyes, it features a
half-dozen statues of saints tucked into niches lined with
ruby-colored cloth. The adjacent museum is notable for
its vestments, barrel organ used to woo the Indians, a

pair of 6-foot-high torches, and a big music stand that supported heavy volumes of Gregorian chants. Other rooms showcase the complete kitchen and adjacent smoke room, displays of Indian artifacts, mid-nineteenth-century furniture, and a Pony Express mail pouch.

Managed by the state Department of Parks and Recreation, San Juan Bautista's historic pueblo character has recently been enhanced by relocating main street utilities underground and installing gas lanterns. The plaza district embraces many of the ancillary buildings that were part of mission life; one that attracts a good deal of attention is the mission jail. "The idea of a jail being maintained by the very men who preached forgiveness and charity to the Indians seems to be repulsive to many persons," writes the Rev. John M. Martin. In fact, jailing and flogging were common methods of punishing the Indians. Martin adds that the padres also tried to put the fear of God into the Indians by warning them of the fire and pains of hell. (Unfortunately, this approach didn't always work: after one stern lecture, an Indian neophyte suggested to a friend that it would be a good idea to move on to hell where they were assured all the wood they would ever need to build warming fires.)

If you come at a later hour, or decide to extend your stay, two restaurants worth considering are the **Mariposa House** at Fourth and Mariposa, where you can lunch on the patio, or **Felipe's**, 313 Third Street, which serves Mexican/Salvadoran food. If you have an optional extension in mind, try **Bed and Breakfast San Juan**, a historic home built in 1858. It's located at 315 The Alameda, San Juan Bautista 95045. Phone (408) 623-4101. The owners will be delighted to introduce you to other fascinating attractions in the area.

Yosemite National Park

Sculpted by glaciers, Yosemite Valley is your gateway to the Sierra Nevada. Entering along the Merced River, you'll see some of the park's waterfalls, reflecting streams, and sentinels such as El Capitan and Three Brothers. A small fraction of the 1,190-square-mile park, the valley is a fine hub where you can quickly slip away from peak season crowds to secluded trails, quiet beaches, and Indian caves most visitors never see. Native Americans lived in the park region for more than 2,000 years before the first non-Indians arrived in the valley in 1851.

The valley's many splendors have attracted writers, artists, and photographers from around the world. James Hutchings, an entrepreneur, began promoting the valley, and soon other hotels and residences were built here. As livestock began grazing in the meadow and orchards were planted, conservationists persuaded President Lincoln to grant the Yosemite Valley and the Mariposa Grove of giant sequoias to California as a public trust in 1864. John Muir's subsequent campaign to end devastation of the High Sierra meadows led to the creation of Yosemite National Park in 1890.

Although Yosemite Valley has become a popular place, it is easy to find peace within the park. The wilderness begins just a few minutes from the roadway, and it's possible to have many memorable trails all to yourself. Whether you hike, bike, or tour by car, Yosemite's alpine lakes, wildlife, and stands of giant sequoia will tempt you to pause and ponder. Here, Muir wrote a century ago, "Nature's peace will flow into you as sunshine flows into trees. The winds will blow their freshness into you and the storms their energy while cares will drop off like autumn leaves."

Most visitors come during the summer season, but the park is an excellent choice any time of year. Waterfalls peak in the spring months, and during the fall you'll find plenty of living color amidst the black oaks, quaking aspens, Pacific dogwoods, and maples. In the winter months the Sierra peaks are frosted and there's skating every night at the Curry Village rink in Yosemite Valley. Whenever you come, get oriented at the Visitor Center in Yosemite Village (just follow the signs as you loop around the valley floor). If you've made a wilderness permit reservation, you can pick up your permit at the booth just outside the front door of the Visitor Center. It's also possible to pick up a wilderness permit here on the spot. But in the busy summer season many trails fill up 24 hours in advance. If you haven't reserved a campsite, check for cancellations at the campground reservation office in the Curry Village parking area here, or book on the spot in the off-season. If you have a campground reservation, you may check in at the campground entrance. At the Visitor Center, you can purchase back-country maps and trail books and get detailed information from rangers on routes, trail conditions, and weather. Here you will find specialized books as well as displays covering the geologic history of the park.

Next door, stop in at the Indian Cultural Museum and the Indian Village dedicated to the valley's original inhab-itants. Exhibits commemorate the tribes who lived here for several thousand years before this land became a national park. While you're in the area you may also want to shop for gifts at the Visitor Center or the Ansel Adams Gallery next door. It's a short walk, drive, or shut-tle bus ride to the trail leading to the base of Yosemite Falls. Then it's time to check in. Following dinner you can enjoy a Yosemite Theater show. Among the dramas offered here is "An Evening with John Muir," a one-man performance that tells the story of Muir's last big environ-mental battle—the fight to prevent Yosemite's Hetch Hetchy Valley from being flooded for a San Francisco reservoir. He lost, but to this day conservationists con-tinue working to drain the reservoir and reclaim Hetch Hetchy Valley. The U.S. Interior Department has actually discussed this idea in recent years, much to the chagrin of San Francisco water officials who are certain it will never come to pass. Admission is $3 for adults and $2 for children. No babies.

For a nightcap, why not try the Ahwahnee Hotel, a showplace that looks like an overgrown Swiss chalet. Furnished in an Indian motif, the hotel's 10-foot-high picture windows keep guests in close touch with the surrounding pines, oaks, and granite cliffs. In the Great Lounge are huge fireplaces and wrought iron chande-liers. The writing room is decorated by Robert Boardman

Howard's impressive wall tapestry. The dining room is a unique contribution to California architecture: a 24-foot-high ceiling with sugar pine trestles is supported by granite pillars faced with more pine. You'll find the help far more cordial than it was in the Ahwahnee's formative years. On one visit when Secretary of Commerce Herbert Hoover returned from a day's fishing, a doorman tried (unsuccessfully) to turn the raggedy future president away.

Road and Weather Information: Call (209) 372-0200. Information available 24 hours a day.

Lodging

Yosemite Park and Curry Company Lodgings are booked centrally by calling (209) 252-4848 or writing to the company at 5410 E. Home, Fresno 93727. If you followed the advice in the beginning of this book, you already have a reservation. If you're visiting in the off-season on a weekday, you may be able to arrange rooms through the reservation line on a last-minute basis. When the park is full, the reservation office may be willing to provide you with a few suggestions for lodging near the park. The park's Public Information Office or Visitor Center can provide a list of accommodations outside the park. Call (209) 372-0265 from 9:00 a.m. to 5:00 p.m. Monday through Friday.

Hotel and cottage rooms at the luxurious **Ahwahnee** start around $188 to $208. **Yosemite Lodge** accommodations range from motel-style rooms at $67 to $90 to bathless cabins at $38 to $52. Accommodations at **Curry Village** range from $80 hotel rooms to cabins without bathrooms at $38 to $52 (you share adjacent rest room and shower facilities with other guests). A lovely place to stay is the Victorian era **Wawona Hotel** located on the south side of the park, 27 miles from Yosemite Valley. Rooms here range from $70 to $90. Tent cabins at Curry Village are $30 to $38. In the summer months, the High Sierra camps provide overnight lodging and meals for hikers. Reservations for this popular camp are assigned on a lottery basis during peak season. Substantial dicounts are available on most rooms midweek during nonholiday periods between November and March.

Reservations for five Yosemite Valley campgrounds can be made up to, but not more than, eight weeks in advance through the Mistix reservation system year-round. (619) 452-0150 or (800) 365-2267 in the U.S. and Canada. In addition to the five primary valley camp-grounds for car travelers, one walk-in campground is operated on a nonreservation basis. If the valley is full, **Crane Flat** (June to October) or **Hodgdon Meadow** on Highway 120 west (year-round) are good alternatives that also operate on a reservation basis May through October. **Wawona Campground** on Highway 41 is open on a first-come, first-served basis year-round, and several campgrounds along Tioga Road are open on a first-come, first-served basis in summer. Call the park's 24-hour information service at (209) 372-0264 for an updated report on campground availability. A number of public campgrounds are available near the park on an unre-served basis. Reservations are accepted at **Indian Flat RV Park** in El Portal, 6 miles west of the Yosemite entrance.

Food
In the valley, you can dine informally at the **Yosemite Lodge** or **Curry Village** cafeterias and **Degan's Deli** or the **Hamburger Stand** in Yosemite Village. The **Four Seasons Restaurant** at the lodge offers breakfast (sea-sonally) and dinner ranging from hamburgers to prime rib. For lobster and broiled steaks, try the **Mountain Room Broiler**. The terrace of the **Mountain Room Bar** is a good spot for a drink during the summer months. One of California's busiest restaurants is found at the **Ahwahnee**. Breakfast (moderate) is a good time to enjoy the picture window views of Glacier Point, Yosemite Falls, and the grassy meadow. Reservations are not required; expect to pay $8 to $15. Dinner (expensive) is by reservation only. (209) 372-1489.

DAY 11
YOSEMITE NATIONAL PARK

After breakfasting at the Ahwahnee Hotel, you'll have a chance to see the best of Yosemite Valley. A bike ride takes you to Happy Isles, where you'll hike the Vernal Falls Trail and then continue to Mirror Lake for lunch. In the afternoon, head for a secluded beach near the Merced River. Or, if you prefer, go for a swim at the Yosemite Lodge pool.

Suggested Schedule	
8:00 a.m.	Breakfast at the Ahwahnee.
9:00 a.m.	Rent a bike at Yosemite Lodge.
9:30 a.m.	Happy Isles Nature Center.
10:00 a.m.	Hike to Vernal Falls Bridge.
12:00 noon	Lunch at Mirror Lake.
1:30 p.m.	Visit Sentinel Beach or swim at Yosemite Lodge Pool.
Evening	Ranger talk or Yosemite Theater.

Travel Route
Rent a bike from the stand at Yosemite Lodge or Curry Village and ride east along the valley floor on the bikeway (or hike if you prefer). Follow the signs toward Happy Isles. After visiting the nature center, hike the trail to Vernal Falls Bridge. After returning to Happy Isles, follow the bike trail to Mirror Lake. From here return west to Yosemite Lodge or Curry Village and return your bike. Then hike west from Yosemite Lodge along the meadow until you reach a bridge over the Merced River. Cross it to the south and walk west along the river until you reach Sentinel Beach (where there's a picnic area). Finally retrace your route to Yosemite Lodge. If you're staying at Curry Village or one of the campgrounds, pick up the shuttle bus in front of Yosemite Lodge.

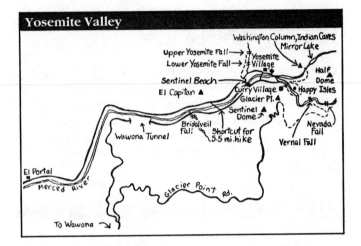

Yosemite Valley

Sightseeing Highlights

▲▲**Happy Isles Nature Center**—One of the most popular and relaxed bike trips in the park leads to Happy Isles Bridge at the beginning of the Nevada Falls Trail. The falls were named by park guardian W. E. Dennisson, who wrote in 1885 that "no one can visit them without for the while forgetting the grinding strife of his world and being happy." The nature center introduces you to park wildlife and vegetation and some of Yosemite's 247 bird species. In the morning the bridge over the Merced River is an excellent picture-taking spot. Sit a while and you may spot mule deer, coyotes, dippers, and butterflies.

▲▲**Vernal Falls**—The start of the 221-mile John Muir Trail extending to Mt. Whitney in Sequoia-Kings Canyon National Park. This is one of the valley's most popular hikes. The first 0.8 mile (moderate) takes you to a bridge where you can get an excellent view of the falls. From here the strenuous 0.7-mile Mist Trail leads up to the top of the falls. In the mid-nineteenth century, hikers made their way to the top of the falls via ladders; today there is an easier route, 500 rock steps. The spray will cool you down on the way up, but bear in mind that the trail is slippery. Keep a close eye on children and use the handrails. Allow an hour for a round-trip to the bridge or two to four hours to complete the round-trip to the top of Vernal Falls. This hike can be extended into a strenuous all-day (3.4-mile) trip to the top of Nevada Falls. An easier way to see the same scenery is to hike down via the Panorama Trail beginning at Glacier Point (see Day 12 for details).

▲▲**Mirror Lake**—A paved trail leads you along the west side of Tenaya Creek to this small reflecting lake. Formed by rock slides from the cliffs above the dammed creek, the lake reflects Half Dome and the surrounding peaks. During the fall this is one of the best spots in the park to see the black oak turn yellow. The trail to the lake is wheelchair-accessible with assistance. However, the 3-mile loop trail around the lake is not wheelchair accessible.

▲▲**Sentinel Beach**—While Yosemite Village and Curry Village can be busy, it doesn't take long to find a quiet retreat. One of the best is just 30 minutes from Yosemite Lodge. Seldom busy, this spot gives you a splendid view of the Three Brothers. The Indians called these peaks "Kom-po-pai-zes," which roughly translates to "mountains playing leapfrog." Sentinel Beach is an ideal place to swim, sunbathe, or simply enjoy views of the sheer rock walls, waterfalls, wildflowers, and mixed-conifer forests. It's also accessible by car from Southside Drive.

Itinerary Option
One of the best flat hikes in Yosemite, easily accessible to visitors, is the 13-mile valley loop beginning at Sunnyside walk-in campground near Yosemite Lodge. This trail parallels the river and Northside Drive and then loops back at Valley View and Southside Drive. You can cut off to Bridalveil Falls before continuing back to Yosemite Lodge. Although there is highway noise along portions of the route, this is one of the least crowded trails in the valley, offering a chance to visit park wilderness missed by most visitors. Much of the scenery equals that of the remote backcountry regions sought out by experienced hikers. To scale the loop back to 5.5 miles, cut off the trail at El Capitan Meadow and take the bridge

across the river. Walk across South-side Drive and continue south until you rejoin the eastbound trail (this shortcut is only marked as a road on the map and you may want to consult a ranger in advance). The shortened 5.5-mile valley loop is well within the reach of the average walker who does not want to scramble up and down waterfall trails. Allow all day for the long hike and about three to four hours for the shorter trip.

Important Note: Before beginning any hike at Yosemite, stop at the Visitor Center for maps, route information, a weather forecast, and reports on any rockslides or other obstacles that could affect your outing. If you have any questions about the difficulty ratings on these trails, discuss them with the ranger. Some guided hikes are available for those who prefer the company of a naturalist who knows the territory. These are listed in the *Yosemite Guide* newspaper available at the Visitor Center or entrance stations.

YOSEMITE NATIONAL PARK

Today's Yosemite itinerary begins with a visit to the giant sequoia grove, followed by a stop at the Pioneer Yosemite History Center. After lunch at a charming old hotel, you'll head over to Glacier Point for one of the best short hikes in the park. Then return to the valley for dinner and a leisurely evening.

Suggested Schedule

8:30 a.m.	Leave Yosemite Valley.
9:30 a.m.	Mariposa Grove.
11:00 a.m.	Pioneer Yosemite History Center.
12:00 noon	Lunch at the Wawona Hotel.
1:30 p.m.	Visit Glacier Point.
2:00 p.m.	Hike to Sentinel Dome.
4:00 p.m.	Return to Yosemite Valley.

Travel Route (102 miles)

Drive west from Yosemite Lodge to Highway 41 south to the Mariposa Grove trailhead (35 miles). After walking or taking the tram tour here, return north to the Pioneer Yosemite History Center at Wawona. Then continue on Highway 41 north to Glacier Point Road. Turn right and drive 16 miles to Glacier Point. Return on this road 2.3 miles to the parking lot at the Sentinel Dome trailhead. After completing this hike, take Glacier Point Road to Highway 41 north and retrace your route back to Yosemite Valley.

Sightseeing Highlights

▲▲▲**Mariposa Grove**—Once found across America, the giant sequoias now exist only in the Sierra Nevada. Older than the giant redwoods found on California's north coast, this species is the largest living thing on earth. Relatively fast growing throughout its life, the giant sequoia lives for several thousand years. At the Mariposa Grove, located near Yosemite's south entrance, is the

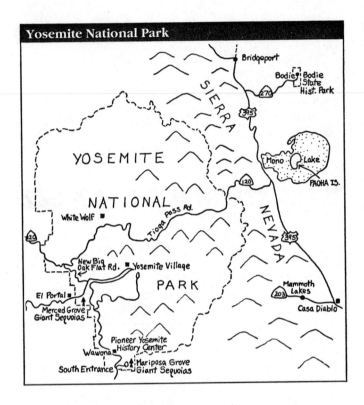

largest sequoia stand in the park. (In the summer months, there is a free shuttle bus service to Mariposa Grove from Wawona and a paid tour bus from Yosemite Valley. Inquire at the visitor center.) You can visit via a tram tour May 1 to October 15 ($6 for adults, $3 for children) or hike amid these vast trees with russet-hued bark. In the winter months, the grove is popular with cross-country skiers.

Along the trail you'll see the Fallen Monarch, California Tree, Wawona Tunnel Tree, and Mariposa Grove Museum. The latter is located inside a small building on the site of a cabin built in 1864 by the Yosemite Grant's first guardian, Galen Clark. Old age does not seem to hurt these remarkably fire-resistant trees: black scars on many of the trunks demonstrate their ability to survive fires that have consumed weaker species. They will continue to grow until wind, snow, and soggy soil ultimately cause them to topple over. These trees, which were here hundreds of years before the birth of Christ, are a major part of the Yosemite legacy. Don't miss the 2,700-year-old Grizzly Giant, the largest tree in the park and one of the world's largest giant sequoias: in 1942, this tree survived six lightning strikes in a single storm.

▲▲**Pioneer Yosemite History Center, Wawona**— Under government protection since 1864, Yosemite Valley and the Mariposa Grove were the cornerstones of this national park founded in 1890. At the Pioneer Center you can visit a dozen historic Yosemite buildings including cabins, shops, and an old jail. Through the living history program (summer only) you'll get a chance to learn about nineteenth-century day-to-day life. Craft and cooking demonstrations are also scheduled here. Be sure to catch a ride in one of the horse-drawn stagecoaches. Don't miss the Wawona Hotel, where you can sit out on the veranda and watch deer explore the golf course. One of California's oldest mountain resorts, it opened for business in 1876 and operates from mid-spring to early fall.

▲▲▲**Glacier Point**—One of Yosemite's most famous promontories. John Muir made instant conservationists out of politicians by bringing them to this overlook. They were overwhelmed by the sheer 3,200-foot drop into Yosemite Valley. You will be too. The view includes landmarks like Half Dome, El Capitan, and the full length of Yosemite Falls. This is a fine place to watch the sunset, and many visitors like to come on full-moon nights. Stargazing here is terrific.

▲▲**Sentinel Dome**—Most Yosemite visitors miss this granite landmark topped by a gnarled Jeffrey pine. It's easily reached via a one-mile hike from the parking area on Glacier Point Road (about 0.5 mile after marker G9 as you return to Highway 41). Your reward for this walk and brief, fairly steep climb to the top of the dome is a 360-degree view of Yosemite, one of the best in the Sierras. (Don't forget to bring your camera.) Another easy hike from the same parking lot leads to the Taft Point Overlook.

Itinerary Option

The Panorama Trail, an all-day downhill hike from Glacier Point, takes you past Illilouette, Nevada, and Vernal Falls to Happy Isles. The 8.5-mile route along the Panorama Cliffs takes four to six hours and is rated moderate with some steep stretches. The easiest way to reach this trail is to take the 8:30 a.m. park bus from Yosemite Lodge to Glacier Point (about one hour) to begin your hike. Confirm the bus schedule the night before because it is subject to change. This is a fair-weather hike: review conditions at the park visitor center before heading out. The rangers can suggest many good alternatives if you'd like to try another hike in the park.

Optional Extension: Mono Lake and Bodie (108 miles from Yosemite)

Highway 120 east, the Tioga Pass Road (open late spring to early fall), takes you across the east side of the park to U.S. 395. Shortly after passing through Lee Vining you'll come to mountain-rimmed Mono Lake. In existence for over 700,000 years, this is one of the oldest lakes in the world. Because it has no outlet, Mono Lake is actually saltier than the ocean: thousands of years of evaporation have concentrated the water's mineral content, making it particularly alkaline. Diversion of tributaries by the Los Angeles Department of Water and Power has reduced the lake's size in recent years and further increased its salinity. In addition, water diversion has turned one of the lake's two islands, Negit, into a peninsula. Once a major rookery for the California gull, this island is now exposed to coyotes who attack the nesting birds. Conservationists are working to stabilize this 13-mile-wide, 8-mile-long lake and preserve its unique environment.

From Mono Lake, continue north on U.S. 395 for 20 miles to S.R. 270. Turn right for the 13-mile drive to Bodie, the best ghost town in California. (The last 3 miles are dirt; the road is closed in winter.)

In the summer of 1932, the entire population of this destitute mining town pulled up stakes and left en masse Because of its remote location, it was spared the looting common in deserted towns of this time. In 1962, the town was declared a state park, ensuring that this time warp would be left intact. Today ghost town aficionados approach the place with the zeal of Renaissance art majors on their first trip to Florence. The state has not developed a motel, put in a gas station, opened a store, or licensed even one hot-dog stand. All you'll find in Bodie are drinking fountains, seventy-five splendidly preserved russet-colored wooden structures, the Standard Mine, and a cemetery. You'll see students' papers still lying on school desktops, homes with their original furniture, glasses still set up on bars, and apothecary bottles filling the drugstore windows.

Although it's quiet today, Bodie is remembered more for its rough-and-tumble life-style than for its gold and silver. "A sea of sin lashed by the tempest of lust and passion," was the way one minister characterized this town that had sixty-five saloons to serve the 10,000 residents who worked 700 mining claims here during its late 1870s heyday. Daily killings were tolled on the fire bell; robberies, stage holdups, and street fights became so commonplace that townspeople frequently turned the other way. When the parents of one young Aurora girl told her they were moving to Bodie, she ended her nighttime prayers by saying, "Good-bye, God, I'm going to Bodie." Today preservationists around the state are working to block a Canadian company eager to resume gold mining at Bodie. They believe this venture would destroy the character of one of California's more fascinating landmarks.

After visiting here, you can spend the night at a Lee Vining motel or one of the resorts in the June Lake area 12 miles south on U.S. 395. There is also camping near Bridgeport at Mill Creek County Park on Lundy Lake 4 miles west of U.S. 395. (619) 932-7911. Sites are $4. No hookups.

Take Highway 120 west the following day and rejoin the main itinerary in the gold country on Day 13.

GOLD RUSH COUNTRY

Although most of urban California is located in the coastal zone, the state's first big boom was in the Mother Lode. Today you'll see some of the towns that drew miners from such disparate points as Germany, China, Brazil, and Boston. Like the Argonauts who came here to make their fortune, the modern-day visitor can expect plenty of excitement in this region that struck it rich with Sutter and was immortalized by Mark Twain and Bret Harte. Along the way, you'll see several historic gold rush towns, tour a mine, visit a railway museum, and spend the night at a century-old hotel.

Suggested Schedule	
8:30 a.m.	Leave Yosemite.
10:00 a.m.	Visit Chinese Camp.
10:30 a.m.	Visit Railtown 1897.
12:00 noon	Lunch in Jamestown.
1:30 p.m.	Check in to your Columbia hotel.
2:00 p.m.	Tour gold mine.
3:00 p.m.	Explore Columbia.
4:00 p.m.	Horseback or stagecoach ride in Columbia.
6:00 p.m.	Dinner.
Evening	Fallon Theater Drama.

Travel Route: Yosemite to Columbia (77 miles)
Take Highway 120 west to Moccasin where the road joins Highway 49 north to Chinese Camp and Jamestown. Continue 2.5 miles north of Sonora on Highway 49 and turn right 3 miles on E18 (Parrots Ferry Road) to Columbia.

The Gold Country
Explorer, politician, and entrepreneur John C. Fremont once observed, "When I came to California, I hadn't a cent. Now I owe two million dollars." Fremont was one of the Forty-Niners who rushed to the Sierra Nevada

foothills in the wake of James Marshall's discovery of gold near the small town of Coloma, about 35 miles northeast of Sacramento, in January 1848. Like many other Forty-Niners, Fremont ended up hopelessly in debt. Although his Mariposa mines at the southern end of the Mother Lode were productive, expenses overtook profits and he was forced to sell them at a fraction of their value.

Despite the long odds, Marshall's lucky strike on the American River changed the face of California. In 1848, the state's population was just 14,000—and only 2,000 of those were Americans who had made the difficult overland journey west. Four years later, the population had jumped to 264,000. Most of that growth was in the gold country, a region centered around 300-mile-long Highway 49. Just about everyone who could walk headed for the hills or seriously considered it. Sailors jumped ship when their vessels docked in San Francisco. Jailers headed off with prisoners in tow to work the mines. Newspapers shut down as reporters and editors headed out of town with shovels and pickaxes.

Today it is hard to imagine that this peaceful region of oak-studded foothills, alpine forests, and deep river gorges was once California's population center: the gold country attracts fewer visitors in a year than Disneyland draws in two weeks. But in its heyday there was no wilder place and gold fever was the order of the day. The crowds of hungry, desperate miners are gone now— although a few people still pan for gold in the region's rivers. But the ghosts of the short-lived society that transformed California and the American West have survived handsomely in the gold country. Left behind after the boom fizzled were mining structures, fancy hotels, covered bridges, and picturesque towns that still tell the story of those turbulent times.

Sightseeing Highlights

▲**Chinese Camp**—This semi-ghost town was once home to about 4,500 miners. Today only about 125 people remain. A number of stone-walled buildings with iron

doors can be seen here, including the Wells Fargo
Building and the Kiwo (General) Store. Take some time
to stroll the quiet streets of this town that is a kind of living memorial to the Chinese who contributed much to
the building of this state.

▲▲**Railtown 1897 State Historic Park, Jamestown**—
Home base of the Sierra Railroad, which operates weekend excursion rail trips from April through November,
this state park has an impressive collection of antique rail
equipment. The trains have been used in over 100
movies and television shows including *High Noon,
Cannery Row, Pale Rider, My Little Chickadee,* and *Back
to the Future III.* The roundhouse, history room, antique
carriage collection, and movie theater are open for tours
daily from May through September and weekends the
rest of the year. Highlights include a rare 1919 Model T
mounted on rail wheels. It had many uses, including
inspection car and ambulance. On payday, the paymaster
and a guard armed with a shotgun drove it down the line
handing out cash. After a picnic lunch, you may want to
visit historic Jamestown. Excursion trains operate on
weekends from March through November. Call (209)
984-3953 for reservations.

▲▲**Columbia State Historic Park**—One of the most
prosperous towns in the Mother Lode, Columbia was the
hub of an $87-million gold mining district. More than
3,000 people lived here in the town's heyday, the 1850s.
When the easily reached placer gold played out, this
community went into a long decline. In 1945, the state
began restoring many of the old buildings, including the
harness shop, barber shop, hotel, two-story brick school-
house, and the Wells Fargo Express Office with its huge
gold scales. Determined to make Columbia a "living community," private tenants were secured to operate candy
and mercantile stores, selling the kind of merchandise
you might find in the 1850-1870 period. Main Street is
closed to traffic during the day, making the town a pleasant place to stroll.

The town's commercial blocks are filled with live
entertainment. Depending on when you visit, you might

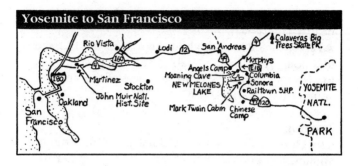

Yosemite to San Francisco

see scruffy Forty-Niners fighting it out in the street or
be entertained from the bandstand next to the City
Hotel. These impromptu performances are all part of
Columbia's gold camp atmosphere. Begin your visit
here on Main Street at the small Columbia Museum,
and then see such highlights as the City Hotel, the
Fallon House, Chinese herb shop, dentist's office, drugstore and fire house. Nearby within easy walking distance are the Church of the Forty-Niners and historic St.
Anne's Catholic Church. At the annual Fireman's Muster,
usually the first weekend in May, the volunteer crew
demonstrates the Papeete Fire Engine, a hand-pumper
made in Boston for the king of the Sandwich Islands;
local firefighters shopping for a unit more than a century
ago in San Francisco found that it was awaiting ship-
ment across the Pacific. They quickly fell in love with
the ornate engine and the beautiful maidens painted on
its side. The Sonora men bought the engine and took it
home to Columbia, where its fire extinguishing power
is demonstrated on weekends. Call (209) 532-0150 for
park information.

▲▲**Hidden Treasure Mine Tour**—This hour-long trip
gives you a chance to go deep inside a hard-rock mine
near Columbia. This is one of the few mines open to the
public. The tour costs $6. It leaves from the Matelot
Gulch Mine Supply Store, Main and Washington streets.
Call (209) 532-9693.

▲▲**Gold Panning**—Learn how to pan for real gold in
the sluice adjacent to the Matelot Gulch Mine Supply
Store: you'll come home with a small vial of gold flakes.

A must for children. Gold panning is also available in nearby Jamestown.

▲**Horseback Ride**—Trail rides ranging from 15 minutes to 2 hours start from the stables near the town parking lot. Here's a good chance to see some of the surrounding countryside. (209) 532-0663.

Lodging

City Hotel, P.O. Box 1870, Columbia 95310, is run in conjunction with Columbia Community College. This gold rush era building is in an ideal location, with nine handsome rooms including two with private balconies overlooking Main Street. Continental breakfast includes freshly baked nut-and-fruit breads, muffins, and rolls from the kitchen's bakery. What Cheer saloon here, with a cherrywood bar shipped around Cape Horn from New England, is a good place for a drink. Room rates range from about $70 to $90. (209) 532-1479.

Fallon House, Columbia (same mailing address as City Hotel above) is another fine old Victorian with beautiful antiques. There's a special room for disabled persons. The theater next door offers repertory drama during the summer and on weekends, Thursdays through Sundays, from September through May. (209) 532-1470.

Ryan House Bed and Breakfast is located at 153 South Shepherd Street, Sonora 95370. This 1850s home with rose-lined walkways is just a short walk from the historic downtown area. Room rates range from $85 to $150. (209) 533-3445.

At **Gunn House**, 286 South Washington, Sonora 95370, all rooms are furnished with antiques in this pioneer adobe building. There's a delightful bar here and a swimming pool, too. Rooms on the back side are quieter. About $45 to $75. (209) 532-3421.

Llamahall Guest Ranch, 18170 Wards Ferry Road, Sonora 95370, a short drive from Sonora, is a working llama ranch in a lovely country setting. Children love this one. About $100. (209) 532-7264.

Campers: Marble Quarry Resort, P.O. Box 850, Columbia 95310, is located a half mile north of Columbia on Italian Bar Road, close to the Stanislaus River Canyon. Sites run $20 to $22. (209) 532-9539.

Food

Students under the direction of the Columbia College Hospitality Management program do a fine job at the **City Hotel** in Columbia. The international menu features escargot, Caesar salad, and grilled and roast duck. Reservations are a must. (209) 532-1479.

Mexican food in the Mother Lode? You bet. The cuisine at **Smoke Café**, 18228 Main Street, Jamestown, is popular with locals and prices here are moderate. (209) 984-3733.

Itinerary Option: Sonora

Just 5 miles from Columbia is the seat of Tuolumne County, Sonora. Begin your tour at the Tuolumne County Museum, 158 West Bradford Avenue. Open from 9:00 a.m. to 4:30 p.m. Monday, Wednesday, and Friday; 10:00 a.m. to 3:30 p.m. Tuesday and Thursday; and 10:00 a.m. to 3:30 p.m. Saturday and Sunday from Memorial Day to Labor Day. It's also the local Chamber of Commerce office. After seeing the museum, including the old jail, pick up a brochure that will guide you on a walking tour of this hilly town. Homes on the tour, such as the Street-Morgan Mansion, a Queen Anne Victorian at 23 West Snell Street, are not open to the public, but you can visit a number of small museums such as the one at St. James Episcopal Church, the red-frame Gothic building that's been a California landmark since 1860. It's open 9:00 a.m. to 1:00 p.m. Monday through Friday. The Sonora Fire Department Museum is also open 9:00 a.m. to 5:00 p.m. daily. To contact the Tuolumne County Visitors Bureau, call (209) 533-4420 or (800) 446-1333, or write to P.O. Box 4020, Sonora 95370.

Optional Extension: Northern Gold Country, Lake Tahoe, and Sacramento

If your visit to Yosemite and the central Mother Lode has you hooked on this region, consider adding a few days.

You can enjoy more of the Mother Lode, see the site of the famous Donner Party tragedy of 1846, and enjoy the alpine splendor of Lake Tahoe. One of the state's most popular mountain destinations, the lake district is a skiing hub and is particularly inviting in the late spring and early fall.

Getting There: This extension leaves the main route at San Andreas and continues north on S.R. 49 to Nevada City. Then drive east on S.R. 20 and Interstate 80 to Truckee where you take S.R. 89 or 267 south to Lake Tahoe. Total distance is about 200 miles. Allow a minimum of three days for this trip. Plan to spend the first night in the Nevada City/Grass Valley area, the second night in Tahoe, and then to return to San Francisco where you will rejoin the main itinerary. A second day in the Tahoe area will give you a more relaxed visit. If you have more time you may want to take the 27-mile drive east on U.S. 50 and S.R. 341 north to the old mining town of Virginia City, Nevada.

An alternative to this route is available to travelers who took the extension from Yosemite to Mono Lake and Bodie. From here U.S. 395 and S.R. 89 north lead to the Tahoe area. Since S.R. 89 is closed in the winter and not recommended for trucks and campers, you may want to take U.S. 395 north to U.S. 50 and then head west to the lake. From Tahoe, it's another 200 miles back to San Francisco via Sacramento. Leave the north shore of Lake Tahoe on S.R. 89 or 267 north to Truckee. Then pick up Interstate 80 west. From the south side take U.S. 50 west to Sacramento where you pick up Interstate 80 west. A slower and very enjoyable way to make the same trip is to take Interstate 80 to S.R. 20 west and the Nevada City/ Grass Valley area. Then pick up S.R. 49 south to Auburn where you follow Interstate 80 back to Sacramento and the Bay Area.

What to See: As you make your way north in the Mother Lode, you'll want to stop at Coloma to visit the Marshall Gold Discovery State Historic Park. It's located 53 miles north of San Andreas on S.R. 49. Continuing north through Auburn you'll reach the Grass Valley/

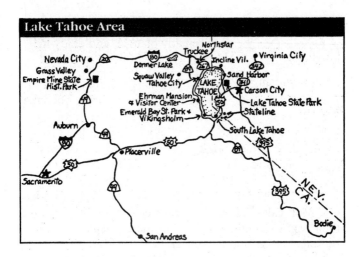

Lake Tahoe Area

Nevada City area. Although hundreds of miles of mine tunnels beneath these two towns are closed, it is still possible to visit the one-time star producer, the Empire North Star Mine. It's part of the Empire Mine State Historic Park on the edge of Grass Valley. The stone office buildings, stamp mills, and mining equipment can all be seen here (the mine closed in 1956). The mansion of Empire owner William Bourn, Jr., was designed by Willis Polk, the noted San Francisco architect, and considered the Xanadu of the Mother Lode. Bourn's estate is a fairyland of sunken and formal gardens, waterfalls, pools, and tennis courts. Among the regular guests was Herbert Hoover, who learned the mining business here. The park is open 9:00 a.m. to 6:00 p.m. daily from April through September, 10:00 a.m. to 5:00 p.m. during the balance of the year. 10791 East Empire Street, (916) 273-8522.

The powerhouse of the nearby North Star Mine—now a museum—has an outstanding collection of Pelton wheels, skips, assay labs, and other mining memorabilia. The North Star Mine had a 12,500-foot shaft, the second deepest in America. Julia Morgan designed the house of manager A. D. Foote; Wallace Stegner fans will recognize it as the setting for his novel, *Angle of Repose*.

After visiting the towns of Grass Valley and Nevada City, continue on S.R. 20 west and Interstate 80 east to Donner Lake. The Donner State Memorial here tells the story of the famous emigrant party trapped at this spot in an early fall 1846 snowstorm. This museum is part of Donner State Park, an excellent place to camp. The lake is warm enough for swimming in the summer months.

From Donner Lake, it's only about half an hour to Lake Tahoe, which boasts 22-million acre-feet of water, 23 campgrounds, 11 stables, 36 public beaches, 19 ski areas, 23 marinas, 10 boat-cruise companies, and the world's largest collection of slot machines (2,250) under one roof. Lake Tahoe's first tourists, fortune hunters on their way to Virginia City's silver mines, began arriving by stage, mule, and horseback in 1860. Mark Twain once suggested that "three months of camp life on Lake Tahoe would restore an Egyptian mummy to his pristine vigor and give him an appetite like an alligator." For those of us who have less time, the lake remains an excellent place to escape to. Certainly that was what some of Tahoe's early families had in mind.

Among them were the Ehrmans, who built a three-story gabled mansion on the west side of the lake. This shingled home with a commanding view of the lake has been incorporated into Sugar Pine Point State Park on the west shore. Guided tours of the mansion are offered during the summer; the park is open all year. Equally impressive but a little harder to reach is Vikingsholm, the replica of an old Norse fortress at Emerald Bay State Park. From South Lake Tahoe you can reach this spot on either the M.S. *Dixie* or an old stern-wheeler called the *Tahoe Queen*. Alternatively, you can hike down the mile-long trail from S.R. 89. A showplace of early Scandinavian architecture, Vikingsholm is a world of turreted towers, stone fireplaces, sod roofs, and dragon crosses. It's open daily 10:00 a.m. to 4:00 p.m., July 1 to Labor Day. Also in this area are the historic Tallac estates, where you can see a number of other early-day mansions including Valhalla, a rustic summer home built by Walter Heller.

While casinos dominate the landscape in Stateline, Nevada, on the south shore, there are a variety of lakefront resorts, condos, and inexpensive motels in this community and adjacent South Lake Tahoe, California. One of the things I like about visiting this region is the variety. Kids can splash in the pool or dig at the lakefront beach in the morning. In the afternoon, a beautiful drive south on S.R. 89 offers easy access to the Hope, Faith, and Charity valleys. Nearby there's also good fishing at the Blue Lakes. Another possibility is Grover Hot Springs State Park, 3.5 miles east of Markleeville. In a meadow at the base of the two bare granite peaks, this spot is popular with backpackers who come to relieve their aches and pains.

One of the nicest beaches in the area is Sand Harbor on the east shore in Lake Tahoe State Park. Located a few minutes south of the Ponderosa Ranch, this beach is the perfect place to picnic or sunbathe. The park also offers fishing along Hidden Beach and hiking to remote spots such as Marlette Lake.

Where to Stay: If your idea of roughing it is a full-service hotel where the help brings you a towel and a chaise longue at the beach, consider the **Hyatt Lake Tahoe** at Incline Village. Rooms start at $199 in the summer and $149 the rest of the year. Check for special packages in the off-season. (702) 831-1111. Another good choice is **Northstar at Tahoe**, 6 miles northwest of Kings Beach and 7 miles southeast of Truckee on S.R. 267. Full resort facilities here start at just $99. Condos are also available. (916) 562-1113. A B&B at Tahoe City on the north shore is the **Mayfield House**, 236 Grove Street, (916) 583-1001. Rooms start around $85. One of my favorite Tahoe B & B's is the $95- to $110-a-night **Chaney House** at 4725 West Lake Blvd. Just steps from the lake, this retreat is a great choice year round. (916) 525-7333. In South Lake Tahoe, **Lakeland Village** at 3535 Lake Tahoe Boulevard offers units starting at $85. Full resort facilities. (916) 541-7711. At Donner Lake, **Donner Country Inn** on Donner Lake Road has B&B units beginning at $95. You can swim, fish, and rent canoes and boats. (916) 587-5574. For more information, contact the Tahoe North Visitors and Convention Bureau at (800) 824-6348; alternatively, try (916) 583-3494. The Lake Tahoe Visitors Authority covers South Lake Tahoe: call (800) AT-TAHOE or (916) 544-5050. For additional lodging suggestions in the Nevada City/Grass Valley area, contact the Nevada County Chamber of Commerce at (916) 273-4667 or (800) 752-6222 (California only).

On your way back to the Bay Area, you'll want to stop in Sacramento to visit Sutter's Fort at 27th and L streets. It's near downtown off Business Route Interstate 80 and is open daily 10:00 a.m. to 5:00 p.m. except Thanksgiving, Christmas, and New Year's Day. (916) 445-4209. Then head downtown to visit the State Capitol and Old Sacramento. The latter is a ten-block historic district with numerous museums, shops, and restaurants along the Sacramento River. The highlight here is the California State Railroad Museum, which operates on the same schedule as Sutter's Fort above. A must for rail fans, this outstanding collection includes twenty-two restored locomotives spanning the history of the iron horse. Other equipment includes the circa 1863 C. P. Huntington, a Canadian National Railways Pullman, and a luxurious private car. Some excursion runs are available here. For more information on the railroad museum, call (916) 448-4466. The Old Sacramento Visitors Center is located at 1104 Front Street, (916) 442-7644 (weekends). The Sacramento Convention and Visitors Bureau is at 1421 K Street, Sacramento 95814. (916) 264-7777 (weekdays).

MOANING CAVERN AND MURPHYS

This morning join the spelunking set and explore **Moaning Cavern**, where you can walk or rappel your way down into the illuminated world of marble stalactites and stalagmites. Then head to Murphys, one of the handsomest Mother Lode towns, before driving across the valley to San Francisco.

Suggested Schedule

8:30 a.m.	Drive to Moaning Cavern.
9:00 a.m.	Visit Moaning Cavern.
10:00 a.m.	Drive to Murphys.
12:00 noon	Lunch at Murphys Hotel or picnic in town park.
1:00 p.m.	Drive to San Francisco.
5:00 p.m.	Arrive at your San Francisco hotel.
7:00 p.m.	Cable car to Fisherman's Wharf for dinner.

Travel Route: Columbia to San Francisco via Murphys (161 miles)

Take Route E18 (Parrots Ferry Bridge) north to Moaning Cavern. Continue on E18 to S.R. 4. Turn east (right) for the short drive to Murphys. Return on S.R. 4 to Angels Camp. Take S.R. 49 north (right) to San Andreas where you pick up S.R. 12 west through the valley to the Sacramento River at Rio Vista. Pick up S.R. 160 south (left) to S.R. 4 west. Continue on S.R. 4 to Interstate 80 south. Take the San Francisco-Oakland Bay Bridge exit to San Francisco and your hotel. From here, walk or take a bus or cab to the Powell Street Cable Car line and ride to Fisherman's Wharf. For more information, contact the San Francisco Visitor Center at (415) 391-2000, or stop by their office on the lower level of Hallidie Plaza near the cable car turnaround at Powell and Market.

Sightseeing Highlights

▲▲**Moaning Cavern**—First explored by gold miners in 1851, this is California's largest public cavern. You can choose between descending a long spiral staircase or rappeling down 180 feet, an adventure for those who have no fear of heights. On the 45-minute tour you'll get a look at 300 million years of geologic history and a wide array of limestone statuary. On the 3-hour adventure tour, serious explorers can crawl through the cavern's inner recesses. Along the way you'll learn about the early-day visitors who approached gingerly because of the moaning noise coming from the entrance. The cavern claimed the lives of more than 100 of these early visitors who either fell in or were tossed down to the bottom as far back as 13,000 years ago. Archaeologists believe some of these well-preserved bones are the oldest human remains found to date in our country. Open daily except Christmas Day. Summer, holiday, and weekend hours: 9:00 a.m. to 6:00 p.m. Winter hours: 10:00 a.m. to 5:00 p.m. Adults $5.75; children ages 6 to 12, $2.75. Extra charge for rappeling and adventure tours. All gear and equipment are provided. (209) 736-2708.

▲▲**Murphys**—Walking past the locust-shaded stone and brick buildings here on a quiet morning, you may feel like you are the first person to discover the charms of this Mother Lode community. In fact, Murphys has been a popular retreat for more than a century. Founded in the gold rush, it quickly became one of California's more desirable retreats, attracting the likes of Ulysses S. Grant, Horatio Alger, Jr., and J. Pierpont Morgan. With the richest mines in Calaveras County, Murphys soon turned into a boomtown. Although the business district was destroyed several times by fire, the town was hastily rebuilt. Many landmark gold rush era structures survive, including the Murphys Hotel established in 1856. The Victorian dining room and bar, complete with moose heads, boast fine period decor.

While Murphys is definitely in life's slow lane, it is seldom dull. Across the street from the hotel is the Old-Timers Museum. Open weekends, it has a good collection of memorabilia, mining displays, and pioneer farm implements. Next door is the Peppermint Stick, an old-fashioned ice cream parlor that's hard to resist. One mile north of town is Mercer Caverns, where you can take a 45-minute tour of eight underground rooms adorned with an impressive array of crystalline formations. Two miles farther down on San Domingo Road is Stevenot, one of the the area's better-known wineries.

Be sure to walk down to the town park, just one block from the Murphys Hotel. Streamside tables on Murphys Creek are ideal for a picnic, and children will enjoy prancing about on the bandstand. Of course, no visit to Murphys is complete without a stroll through the residential areas. Along the way, in idyllic settings, you'll see iron doors shuttering stores that have been converted into country homes. You're also likely to meet up with some of the town donkeys, see a Gothic church, and photograph some of Murphys' classy Victorian and Italianate homes. Among them is the Dunbar House, a bed-and-breakfast inn. Murphys is also a popular stop en route to Calaveras Big Trees State Park, about 20 miles northeast on S.R. 4.

Itinerary Option: John Muir House, Martinez
On the final stretch of today's drive, you'll pass by the home and orchards of John Muir, founding father of the Sierra Club, famed author, and diehard conservationist. Take the Alhambra Avenue exit off S.R. 4 to the John Muir National Historic Site. A tour takes you through Muir's 17-room Victorian mansion, including the tower/office where he worked on his books. Visitors can tour the orchards and, in season, sample figs right off the trees. Also on the property is the two-story adobe that was the home of Muir's daughter. A sign warns visitors to evacuate the building in the event of an earthquake because it is not seismically safe. There is no admission charge at this site, open daily 10:00 a.m. to 4:30 p.m. except New Year's Day, Thanksgiving, and Christmas. (415) 228-8860. If you want to add this option, leave Murphys by 12:30 p.m.

San Francisco
Beautifully lit, the Bay Bridge is your gateway to the city that got its start in life as the port of entry to the gold rush. A boomtown in every sense of the word, San Francisco

was California's financial capital at a time when Los Angeles was little more than a cow town fighting for direct rail service. Often lost under a cloud bank, this city has a slightly larger than life quality. There are streets that look like they were designed as slalom courses, parks that extend nearly half the width of the city, and views that literally stop traffic. The magic of San Francisco isn't just the cable cars or Tony Bennett doing a voice-over: what makes this city so special is the proximity of its famous landmarks; you can see a great deal here in just a few days. And, while San Francisco has everything you'd expect in a cultural capital, it is just 20 minutes from coastal wilderness.

Because it's a relatively small city, San Francisco is well suited to a casual visiting style, allowing you to sample many of its highlights without strain. Thanks to all the ferries, cable cars, clubs, interesting shops, big and little museums, plazas, parks, and galleries, it's easy to find a change of pace. Convenient, entertaining, nice to look at, San Francisco is the closest America is likely to get to an urban national park.

Lodging

San Francisco offers a good choice of hotel rooms and bed-and-breakfast and hostel accommodations in all price ranges. Except during major conventions, finding a room should not be difficult. But reservations are advised for the more popular bed-and-breakfast inns and some hotels. Some popular areas, such as Fisherman's Wharf, can fill up during the peak summer tourist season. Many big hotels offer discounts on weekends and during the Christmas holidays. Inquire about these deals when you check in. Price ranges listed are approximate. To guarantee the lowest possible rate, book ahead.

Bed and Breakfasts/Inns: The B&B craze got off to an early start here. If you're partial to B&Bs or European-style inns, or have always wanted to try one, here are some suggestions in San Francisco. They range from Haight-Ashbury classics like the Red Victorian Inn (where you can stay in an attractive unit that's furnished like a '60s crash pad) to the Sherman House, an elegant Pacific

Heights establishment with formal gardens. Scattered around the city, they offer a wide range of choices. Reservations are a must for these establishments.

Located between Chinatown and colorful North Beach, the **Obrero Hotel and Basque Restaurant** at 1208 Stockton Street, 94133, charges $45 for a room and large breakfast. French, German, Italian, and Cantonese are spoken here. (415) 989-3960 mornings and evenings.

In the Fisherman's Wharf area, the **San Remo**, a small historic Victorian hotel at 2237 Mason Street, 94133, offers rooms from $55 to $75. (415) 776-8688. Located on a quiet cul-de-sac in the fashionable Union Street area is the **Bed and Breakfast Inn** at 4 Charlton Court, 94123. The nine rooms range from cozy facilities with shared bath to deluxe accommodations with their own sun deck. Rates range from $70 to $140. (415) 921-9784.

In the Upper Market area, convenient to downtown, the Castro, and Haight-Ashbury, is the **Willows B&B Inn** at 710 14th Street, 94114. Rooms range from $66 to $120. (415) 431-4770. **The Red Victorian**, 1665 Haight Street, 94117, is close to Golden Gate Park and a blast from the Haight-Ashbury past. Rooms range from $55 to $200, (415) 864-1978.

If you're planning to splurge in San Francisco, the most expensive B&B in town is the **Sherman House** at 2160 Green Street, 94123. (415) 563-3600. You'll enjoy a beautiful view of the bay here in Pacific Heights. Rooms range from $250 to $375. Not far away, the **Archbishop's Mansion** at 1000 Fulton, 94117, on handsome Alamo Square offers rooms from $115 to $385. (415) 563-7872. Should you prefer to stay in a private home—anything from a budget apartment to a luxurious Victorian—contact **Bed and Breakfast International**, (415) 696-1690. They have listings of accommodations throughout the San Francisco area and many other parts of California ranging from $60 to $100 per night. Send a self-addressed stamped envelope to 1181-B Solano Avenue, Albany, CA 94706. Another listing service is the **American Family Inn** at P.O. Box 420009, San Francisco 94142. Rooms run $45 to $125 per night. (415) 479-1913. Free brochure available.

Hotels: When she's in town, Queen Elizabeth prefers the understated elegance of the **Huntington Hotel** at 1075 California, 94108. Rooms here range from $160 to $230. (800) 652-1539 within California; (800) 227-4683 outside California; (415) 474-5400. Presidents of the United States and of Coca-Cola stay on Union Square at the **Westin St. Francis**. (Try for a room in the older building.) It's at 335 Powell between Geary and Post, 94102. (800) 228-3000 or (415) 397-7000. Rooms range from $180 to $275.

Park Hyatt at 333 Battery, 94108, has an excellent location in the financial district and also has one of the city's finer restaurants. (415) 392-1234. Rates are from $249 to $325. For those seeking a reasonably priced central location, we recommend Chinatown's **Grant Plaza Hotel** at 465 Grant Avenue, 94109. Rooms on Grant Avenue are quieter than those facing Bush Street. Rates range from $37 to $73. (415) 434-3883 or (800) 472-6899.

On Market Street, the **Sheraton-Palace** at 2 New Montgomery, 94105, is known for its Garden Court where you dine beneath a vast leaded-glass dome and crystal chandeliers. The ambience is reason enough to have breakfast or lunch here. Many political leaders have stayed at the Palace and a few have passed away at this landmark. King David Kalakaua of Hawaii spent the last days of his life here in 1891, as did President Warren Harding in 1923. (415) 392-8600. $159 to $305.

Travelodge Near Ghirardelli Square at 1201 Columbus Avenue, 94133, charges $75 to $95. (800) 255-3050 or (415) 776-7070. At **Howard Johnson's Motor Lodge** at 580 Beach Street, 94133, rooms go for $89 to $139. (800) 645-9258 in California; (800) 654-2000 outside California; (415) 775-3800. The **Holiday Inn Fisherman's Wharf** at 1300 Columbus Avenue, 94133, offers rooms for $105 to $160. (800) HOLIDAY or (415) 771-9000.

Across the Golden Gate Bridge consider the **Casa Madrona Hotel** at 801 Bridgeway, rooms run $105 to $250. (415) 332-0502. Beautiful views make this hillside hotel a winner.

Budget Accommodations: Located at Fort Mason near the bay, the **San Francisco International Youth**

Hostel charges $14 for dormitory-style accommodations. It has community kitchens and a three-night maximum stay. Call (415) 771-7277. IYH also operates other Bay Area hostels.

   Camping: San Francisco R.V. Park, 250 King, at Third Street, 94107. Near downtown. $30 to $36 per night. (415) 986-8730.

Food

There are many reasons why San Francisco is famous for its seafood. One of them is **Yuet Lee**, 1300 Stockton, (415) 982-6020. The clams, squid, crab, and oysters are all winners in this clay-pot citadel. Open until 3:00 a.m., closed Tuesday. Vegetarians will also be at home in this moderately priced restaurant. Nearby in the Financial District is **Sam's Grill**, 374 Bush; (415) 421-0594. The sand dabs come highly recommended at this San Francisco institution. Dining in the wood-paneled private rooms here is a treat, particularly when you consider the moderate prices. Open 11:00 a.m. to 8:30 p.m., closed Saturday and Sunday. **Harbor Village** in #4 Embarcadero Center is a good bet for dim sum, Chinese specialties served off rolling carts. (415) 781-8833.

   Nearby at 240 California Street is **Tadich Grill**, another traditional San Francisco seafood restaurant with handsome booths and moderate prices. (415) 391-1849. Closed weekends. (Consider the counter if you don't want to wait for petrale sole.) Another good seafood establishment is the **Hayes Street Grill** at 320 Hayes Street near Franklin in the Civic Center area. (415) 863-5545. Closed Sunday. Moderately priced; reservations are a good idea. Wolfgang Puck's **Postrio** features dishes like Chinese–style duck with spicy mango sauce and quail with pineapple glaze. It's near Union Square at 545 Post Street. (415) 776-7825. **Bocce Cafe** at 478 Green Street is a favorite with the singles crowd. Ask for a patio table; (415) 981-2044. Garlic lovers will enjoy another North Beach favorite, **Caffe Sport** at 574 Green. (415) 981-1251. I'm also partial to the Mediterranean-inspired food at **Square One**, 190 Pacific Avenue. (415) 788-1110.

In the Fisherman's Wharf area, a good choice for Italian cuisine, seafood, or steak is **Swiss Louis Restaurant**, Pier 39. (415) 421-2913. Moderate prices. One of the best views in the city can be enjoyed from **Paprikas Fono**, a Hungarian restaurant at Ghirardelli Square, 900 North Point, (415) 441-1223. Moderate prices and one of the few places in town where you can enjoy gulyas soup.

In the Civic Center area, the **Zuni Café** at 1658 Market Street serves fine California cuisine. The menu offers seafood, chicken, pasta, great salads, and homemade ice cream in a handsome setting. Closed Monday. (415) 552-2522. The **California Culinary Academy**, a school for chefs, offers well-priced meals in three dining rooms. It's at 625 Polk Street. (415) 771-3500. **Stars** at 150 Redwood Alley is the place to try famed chef Jeremiah Tower's seafood, steaks, and salads. (415) 861-7827. For French cuisine in a casual setting, try **South Park Cafe**, located just three blocks south of Moscone Center at 108 South Park. (415) 495-7275.

Angkor Wat Cambodian Restaurant at 4217 Geary Boulevard in Presidio Heights is one of San Francisco's better Asian dining rooms. Try the green papaya salad, charbroiled beef roll, and chicken salad. There's Cambodian classical dancing Friday and Saturday night. (415) 221-7887. **Buca Giovanni** at 800 Greenwich Street in North Beach is an elegant place to try veal dishes, seafood, or polenta. This is among the city's best Italian cooking. (415) 776-7766. **Greens** in Fort Mason Center's Building A, Marina Boulevard and Laguna Street, is arguably the city's finest vegetarian restaurant. (415) 771-6222. Moderately priced, it's open for lunch Monday through Friday, dinner Tuesday through Saturday, and Sunday brunch. Reservations are a must.

SAN FRANCISCO

From a walk up Telegraph Hill to a stroll through the Marin Headlands, today's itinerary gives you a chance to enjoy the best of the San Francisco area. While other tourists are fighting for a parking spot or queuing up for tour buses, you'll enjoy some of the secrets San Franciscans try to keep to themselves. Here's your chance to scramble through a submarine, see the mansions of fabled Pacific Heights, and cross the Golden Gate Bridge to visit a marine mammal rehabilitation center. You'll be back in time for a chance to shop, dine, and catch a memorable show.

Suggested Schedule

8:30 a.m.	Filbert Steps to Coit Tower.
9:30 a.m.	Drive through North Beach to Fisherman's Wharf.
10:00 a.m.	National Maritime Museum.
11:30 a.m.	Drive through Pacific Heights.
12:30 p.m.	Picnic at Fort Point.
1:00 p.m.	Cross Golden Gate Bridge to Marin Headlands.
2:00 p.m.	Marin Headlands/Sausalito.
5:00 p.m.	Return to your hotel.
6:00 p.m.	Dinner.
8:00 p.m.	Show.

Travel Route: San Francisco to Marin Headlands/ Sausalito (round-trip 30 miles)

Take Sansome Street north across Broadway. Park in the vicinity of Levi Plaza. Walk up the Filbert Stairs to Coit Tower. Retrace your steps or descend via the parallel Greenwich Stairs. Take Sansome to the Embarcadero, turn left and follow it to Bay Street where you turn left again. Take Bay to Columbus and turn right. Turn left on North Point, follow it to Ghirardelli Square, and park below in the garage.

After visiting the maritime museum, drive on North Point to Polk and turn left. Continue to Bay and turn right. At Van Ness, make a left to Jackson where you turn right. Continue to Divisadero and turn right. Turn left on Vallejo two blocks to Baker Street, and turn right to the Palace of Fine Arts. Follow Marina Boulevard to U.S. 101 north, exiting on Lincoln Boulevard north to Fort Point. Return to U.S. 101 north, and cross the Golden Gate Bridge. Take the Alexander Avenue exit to Bunker Road and turn left. Cross under the freeway and through a tunnel to the Marin Headlands at Fort Cronkhite.

To visit Sausalito, return on Bunker Road beneath the freeway, and turn left on Bridgeway Boulevard into Sausalito. Then take Bridgeway back to U.S. 101 south and return to San Francisco.

Sightseeing Highlights
▲▲Coit Tower/Filbert Steps—Most visitors approach Telegraph Hill via Stockton and Lombard streets from North Beach. A better idea—for those who can endure a steep hike—is to take the Filbert Steps, which approach this landmark from the east side. Unfamiliar to many San Franciscans, this handsome walkway is a network of platforms and wooden steps. Your ascent begins at Sansome Street near Levi Plaza. You'll climb past a glorious garden and small wooden houses built during the gold rush era; among them is the handsome Carpenter Gothic at 228 Filbert Steps, a private residence. Other historic wooden homes are seen on adjacent Darrell Place and Napier Lane. This is a demanding climb, but fortunately you can rest at benches along the way. (Inscribed on one of them is, "I have a feeling we're not in Kansas anymore.") At the summit is Coit Tower, San Francisco's exclamation point. A memorial to San Francisco firefighters, this modern-style monument has some fine murals tracing the state's history. From the top you'll enjoy a good panorama of the region. Descend the hill via parallel Greenwich Stairs; or if you prefer, walk down the hill's west side to North Beach and Washington Square. From here it's a short walk on Columbus Avenue to Fisher-

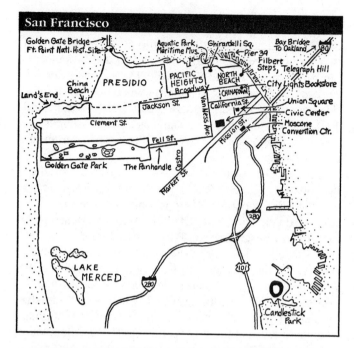

man's Wharf. The #39 Muni bus will also take you from Coit Tower to Fisherman's Wharf. You can return to Levi Plaza on foot or via Muni bus #42 on Bay Street. Get off on Battery Street at Levi Plaza and walk west to Sansome and your car. Or take the 20-minute walk along the Embarcadero back to Battery Street and the Plaza.

▲▲▲**National Maritime Museum/Hyde Street Pier—** The nation's largest fleet of historic vessels is found here at the foot of Hyde Street. In addition to the six ships at this location, you can walk east to the submarine *Pampanito* at Pier 45 or west to the Liberty Ship *Jeremiah O'Brien* docked at Pier 3, Fort Mason. The latter is the last unaltered survivor of the 2,751 Liberty Ships built during World War II. Completed in just six to eight weeks, these ships were a mainstay of our military effort in all theaters. Both the *Pampanito* and the *Jeremiah O'Brien* are National Historic Landmarks. Others include the *Balcutha*, a square-rigged Cape Horn sailing ship launched in 1886; it represents hundreds of vessels that

brought coal, wine, and hardware from Europe to trade
for California grain. Next door is the *C. A. Thayer*, one of
two surviving vessels from a fleet of 900 that brought
lumber from the Pacific Northwest. The side-wheeler
Eureka takes you back to the days when dozens of ferries brightened up San Francisco Bay. Between 1922 and
1941, this vessel brought as many as 2,300 passengers
and 120 autos across the bay in a single trip. Tour all of
these classics.

On the scene—but not accessible to visitors—are the
oceangoing tug *Hercules*, the paddle tug *Eppleton Hall*,
and the scow schooner *Alma*. Just north of the pier,
across Aquatic Park, is the National Maritime Museum
building on Beach Street at Polk. Located inside this
boat-shaped building are exhibits on the city's maritime
history. It's a short walk east from here to Pier 45 and the
Pampanito, a fleet submarine designed for long-range
cruises in the Pacific during World War II. Don't miss the
fascinating tour of this vessel. Don a pair of headphones
to enjoy a tour narrated by World War II crew members.

Important Note: If you're planning to visit Alcatraz,
the first excursion on Day 16, buy your tickets for tomorrow morning's early sailing at Pier 41, located at the foot
of Powell Street, before leaving the wharf area this morning. (415) 546-2896.

The Hyde Street Pier is open daily 10:00 a.m. to 6:00
p.m., (415) 556-6435. The gift shop is a good place to
look for nautical theme souvenirs. The National Maritime
Museum building is open 10:00 a.m. to 6:00 p.m. May
through October, and 10:00 a.m. to 5:00 p.m. November
through April. (415) 556-2904. Both are wheelchair-
accessible. The *Pampanito* is open 9:00 a.m. to 9:00 p.m.
May through September. From October through April, it's
open 9:00 a.m. to 6:00 p.m. Monday through Thursday
and 9:00 a.m. to 9:00 p.m. Friday through Sunday. (415)
929-0202. The *Jeremiah O'Brien* is open daily 9:00 a.m.
to 3:00 p.m. There are also special open-ship weekends
in the summer and fall. (415) 441-3101.

▲▲**Pacific Heights Drive**—A trip along the north
side of the city takes you past the grand Queen Anne,

Italianate, Spanish Renaissance, Eastlake stick-style, and Greek revival mansions of Pacific Heights. Any route west along this hillside is fine, as long as you end up at Baker Street and drive north (right) to the Palace of Fine Arts. A landmark created by famed Berkeley architect Bernard Maybeck for the 1915 Panama-Pacific Exposition, it includes San Francisco's only outdoor Roman rotunda. The park fronting on a small lake here is a good resting spot. The Palace is now the home of the Exploratorium, a superb science museum you may want to visit later. The Exploratorium is open Wednesday to Friday 1:00 to 5:00 p.m., Saturday and Sunday noon to 5:00 p.m., and Wednesday 7:00 to 9:30 p.m. Adults $7; children under 17, $3. (415) 561-0360.

▲▲**Fort Point**—Located near the south anchorage of the Golden Gate Bridge, this brick seacoast fort was completed in 1861; similar in design to Fort Sumter, this garrison was designed to protect the city from surprise attack during the Civil War. Try to make it to the 12:30 p.m. cannon firing. Visit the museum here and then climb upstairs for superb views of the bay and bridge. Open 10:00 a.m. to 5:00 p.m., closed Christmas Day and New Year's Day. Stay on established walkways, keep off walls, and stay close to children. Picnic near the breakwater where you'll enjoy a view of your next destination. (415) 556-1693.

▲▲**Marin Headlands/Fort Cronkhite**—This former military site offers fine hiking along old Miwok Indian trails and Rodeo Beach. A popular short hike leads up from the beach (no swimming) to an old Nike missile site overlooking Rodeo Lagoon. You can also explore old batteries that were part of Fort Cronkhite. Of special interest here is the California Marine Mammal Rehabilitation Center. At this coastal site, wounded seals and other ailing animals are nursed back to health and returned to the sea. If you fall in love with this area and want to spend the night, consider the Golden Gate Hostel located in Building 941, Fort Barry. Lodging costs $8 per night. (415) 331-2777. For information on visiting the Marin Headlands, contact the visitor center at (415) 331-1540.

If you are not driving to Humboldt County's Avenue of the Giants (Day 18), consider returning to U.S. 101 north and taking the S.R. 1 exit in Mill Valley to see the redwoods at Muir Woods National Monument. (415) 388-2595. Open 8:00 a.m. to sunset.

After visiting the Marin Headlands, you may want to drive to Sausalito and explore some of the popular shops along Bridgeway Avenue. The **no-name bar** here or the **Alta Mira Hotel**, with a fine view of the bay, are good places for a drink. My favorite Sausalito attraction is the Bay Model operated by the Army Corps of Engineers. Located at 2100 Bridgeway, it is a working hydraulic model of San Francisco Bay and the Sacramento Delta. Open Tuesday to Saturday from 9:00 a.m. to 4:00 p.m. Admission is free. (415) 332-3870. Kids will enjoy this one.

Nightlife
Stage: The city's longest running (since 1975) musical revue is *Beach Blanket Babylon*. Wild and crazy, with outrageous props, weird costumes, and Carmen Miranda hats, this 90-minute show has become a local institution. (In fact, some people think this cabaret act belongs in one.) At **Club Fugazi**, 678 Green Street, Wednesday and Thursday, 8:00 p.m.; Friday and Saturday, 8:00 p.m. and 10:30 p.m.; Sunday, 3:00 p.m. and 7:30 p.m. Minors under 21 are only allowed at the Sunday matinee. (415) 421-4222. A new club, **Cyril's**, is located downstairs.

The Bay Area has several good repertory companies. One is the **American Conservatory Theater** at 450 Geary Street, (415) 749-2228. Worth a drive or BART ride is the **Berkeley Repertory Theater** at 2025 Addison Street, (510) 845-4700.

Clubs: For jazz, visit **Kimball's** in San Francisco at 300 Grove Street. (415) 861-5555. Another excellent choice is **Yoshi's** at 6030 Claremont Avenue, Oakland. (510) 652-9200. The city also has a number of fine comedy clubs such as **Cobb's** at 2801 Leavenworth. (415) 928-4320. Also popular is the **Holy City Zoo** at 408 Clement Street. (415) 386-4242. For dinner, drinks,

Polynesian-style entertainment, and some interesting special effects, try the Tonga Room at the **Fairmont Hotel**, California and Mason streets. (415) 772-5278. It's built around the hotel's old Olympic-size swimming pool, which is regularly lashed by a man-made tropical storm, complete with ersatz lightning and thunder.

San Francisco has many "top o'" clubs and restaurants such as **Top of the Mark** (Hopkins), the **Carnelian Room** (Bank of America), and the **Equinox** (Hyatt Regency San Francisco). If you're a mystery buff, consider drinking in the view at **Sherlock Holmes, Esq.** atop the Holiday Inn Union Square, 480 Sutter Street, (415) 398-8900. After seeing the glassed-in Sherlock Holmes museum you can enjoy a drink in the traditional British lounge furnished á la Conan Doyle. It's open from 4:00 p.m. to 1:30 a.m. There's live music and, of course, breathtaking views of San Francisco. Next door is the **Persian Slipper Club**, a members-only establishment operated by the Sherlock Holmes Society.

The South of Market area adjacent to downtown has become a hub for new restaurants and clubs. Located in an industrial district, this neighborhood may be the only one in America where you'll spot groups with names like the "Converse All-Star Orchestra" and "Patsy Cline and the Memphis G-Spots." It's calmer today, as the gay bars of yesteryear have been succumbing to a wave of hetero-sexual takeovers. One popular dance club is the **DNA Lounge** at 375 11th Street, (415) 626-1409. **Club DV8** offers a wide variety of bands and special events. It's at 55 Natoma Street, (415) 957-1730. In Haight-Ashbury, the **I-Beam** is a popular disco where you'll find live rock, dancing, video, laser shows, and (on Sunday) tea dancing. It's at 1748 Haight. (415) 668-6006.

ALCATRAZ AND GOLDEN GATE PARK

Today you'll get a chance to visit Alcatraz, just like Al Capone. (The difference is that you have to pay for the boat ride over.) After exploring Golden Gate Park and enjoying a picnic lunch, you'll return to North Beach, visit City Lights bookstore, and walk through Chinatown to Union Square in time for shopping. Enjoy dinner and another night on the town.

Suggested Schedule	
8:45 a.m.	Boat to Alcatraz.
11:30 a.m.	Explore Golden Gate Park.
2:30 p.m.	Drive to North Beach via Seacliff, Clement Street, and Pacific Heights.
3:00 p.m.	Explore North Beach, Chinatown, and Union Square.
Evening	Dinner and show.

Travel Route
Take the Red and White Ferry tour to Alcatraz from Pier 41. Then take Van Ness Avenue south to Fell Street and turn right. Follow Fell to Kennedy Drive, which leads into Golden Gate Park. After picnicking at Stow Lake and exploring the park, head west to the Great Highway. Follow it north (right) to Geary Boulevard and then turn left to Lincoln Park and the Palace of the Legion of Honor. Return along El Camino del Mar to Seacliff Avenue. Turn right on 26th Avenue to Clement Street and turn left. Follow Clement to Arguello and turn left. Turn right on Jackson Street to Fillmore and turn left to Broadway. Continue through the tunnel to North Beach, parking in the vicinity of Columbus (or your hotel if you are staying close to this area). Walk through North Beach, Chinatown, Union Square, and Golden Gate Park.

Sightseeing Highlights
▲▲**Alcatraz**—San Francisco's only island hotel enjoyed almost 100 percent occupancy from opening day in 1934

until it closed in 1963. Providing accommodations on the American plan, Alcatraz had one employee to watch over the needs of every three guests. The 260 long-stay residents enjoyed probably the best cuisine in the federal system. People killed to get in here! High operational costs, deterioration of the old buildings due to harsh weather, and political pressure from Washington and the Bay Area led to the prison's demise. Today it's the "Smithsonian" of penitentiaries, offering a chance to be locked up in solitary confinement and to see the mess hall, the cell blocks, and mementos of famous escape attempts. After arriving, you'll view a 15-minute slide program on the island's history. An hourly ranger program explores the island's cultural history. There's also a self-guided audio-tour that walks you through the military and penal history of this island (which some San Franciscans would now like to turn into a casino). Boats leave Pier 41 daily on a reservation-only basis from 8:45 a.m. to 2:45 p.m. Book at least a day in advance at Pier 41 or by calling Ticketron. The combined ferry service and self-guided audio-tour (you listen to portable wands) featuring narration by former guards and inmates is $8.50 for adults and $4.50 for children. The price drops to $5.50 for adults and $3 for children who don't want to take the audio-tour. There is no charge for the ranger-led walks. Dress warmly and wear sturdy shoes. For information, call (415) 546-2896.

▲▲**Golden Gate Park**—Thanks to landscape architect Frederick Law Olmstead's genius, this former sand dune has been transformed into one of the nation's outstanding urban retreats. Olmstead, who also created New York's Central Park and Oakland's Mountain View Cemetery (even elite San Franciscans like Charles Crocker, one of the Big Four railroad barons, ended up there), wanted this to be a park that would entertain and enlighten the entire city. Following his mandate, the city maintains on this site more than 5,000 kinds of plants, 27 miles of hiking trails, 11 lakes, a 7-mile-long bike path, 2 major museums, a fly-casting pool, a hall of flowers, a pioneer log cabin, a redwood grove, buffalo, elk, and deer paddocks, windmills, tulip gardens, a planetarium,

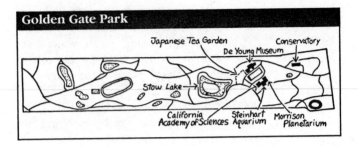

Golden Gate Park

and an aquarium. Most visitors flock to the south end of the park in the vicinity of the De Young Art Museum, the Japanese Tea Garden, and the California Academy of Sciences. Enjoy your picnic lunch at Stow Lake where it's possible to rent pedal or motor boats. There's even an island called Strawberry Hill in the middle of the lake. At the west end of the park you can take the Great Highway past the Cliff House, the ruins of the Sutro Baths, and Point Lobos, to Clement Street and Lincoln Park. Here is the Palace of the Legion of Honor, a museum well worth visiting for its French impressionist paintings and Rodin sculpture. From here you can visit the Seacliff area before returning to North Beach.

▲▲**North Beach/Chinatown**—Once a beach that was buried under landfill, this region is no longer the city's northern boundary. While San Francisco has grown, North Beach has retained a popular assortment of Italian restaurants, cafés, boutiques, bars, and bookstores like **City Lights** at 261 Columbus. Once a second home to the beat generation, this shop has made few concessions to mass marketing. The building, also home base for a publishing company operated by poet Lawrence Ferlinghetti, attracts book lovers from all over the world. Browsers are always welcome. Pull up a chair in the basement and read at your leisure: management doesn't mind if you browse here all afternoon without spending a dime. After exploring North Beach, walk south along Grant Avenue through Chinatown to Post and turn right (west) to Union Square. If you arrive between 3:00 p.m. and 4:30 p.m., stop by the elegant **Compass Rose** bar at the St. Francis Hotel to enjoy afternoon tea. On or near the square are many of the city's leading shops such as Saks, Neiman-Marcus, Gumps, and F.A.O. Schwarz.

Itinerary Options
Angel Island: Accessible from Fisherman's Wharf, this refuge in San Francisco Bay is blessed with fine trails and quiet beaches on weekdays. It's busier on weekends, but still worth a trip. Come for a few hours to relax at this state park, or hike all the way around the island, exploring Battery Wallace, the West Garrison, and the old Nike missile site. Superb views of the Bay Area. For park information, call (415) 435-1915. For ferry information, call (415) 546-2896.

Little Museums: San Francisco has many fine museums like the De Young, the Museum of Modern Art, and the California Academy of Sciences. The Steinhart Aquarium is also delightful. You might also want to see some of the city's lesser-known, but very interesting, small museums. Worth a visit is the Cable Car Museum at 1201 Mason Street; it's open daily from 10:00 a.m. to 6:00 p.m. (415) 474-1887. At Fort Mason, you can visit the Mexican Museum and the Italian-American Museum. Both are open noon to 5:00 p.m. Wednesday through Sunday. Call the Mexican Museum at (415) 441-0404 and the Museo Italo Americano at (415) 673-2200. The Wells Fargo History Museum at 420 Montgomery Street is open Monday through Friday, 9:00 a.m. to 5:00 p.m., closed bank holidays. (415) 396-2619.

Highway 1 to Point Reyes: Take the Golden Gate Bridge to the Highway 1 exit in Mill Valley. Continue to Stinson Beach and the Audubon Canyon Ranch, a 1,000-acre bird sanctuary where the hiking trails offer close encounters with egrets and great blue herons. Located at 4900 Highway 1, it's open weekends and holidays, and during the week by appointment. Call (415) 868-9244. From here you can head north to Point Reyes National Seashore. Although roads lead out to the ocean and to the site where Sir Francis Drake landed the *Golden Hind* in 1579, be sure to take time to enjoy one of the many hiking trails on this 64,000-acre peninsula. A short, infor-

mative walk is the self-guided Earthquake Nature Trail
that begins at the park headquarters, (415) 663-1092, on
Bear Valley Road. Turn left off Highway 1 near Olema
and follow the signs. Geologically, Point Reyes is an
island separated from the mainland by the San Andreas
Fault: as a result, rocks on the peninsula are totally different from those on the mainland. During the 1906 earthquake, the land on Point Reyes shifted northward as
much as 21 feet. You can see excellent visual evidence
of this shift on the Earthquake Trail.

From the park headquarters take Bear Valley Road to
Limantour Road for the 8-mile ride out to Limantour
Beach and Drake's Bay. Another wonderful spot is
Heart's Desire Beach in Tomales Bay State Park west of
Inverness. Return to San Francisco via Point Reyes
Station. Take Point Reyes-Petaluma Road north to Nicasio
Valley Road and turn right. Pick up Lucas Valley Road a
mile east of Nicasio. You'll pass film magnate George
Lucas's studio as you continue east to U.S. 101 south in
San Rafael. Allow all day for the round-trip. (Or, if you
prefer, head north on U.S. 101, picking up the Day 17
itinerary.)

Russian River: North of Santa Rosa along Route 116
is the popular Russian River. I'm partial to the **Highland
Dell Inn** at 21050 River Boulevard in Monte Rio (707-
865-1759). Rooms at this B&B run $70 to $225 a night.
Applewood, an estate inn in the same area, is another
winner (13555 Highway 116, 707-869-9093). Rooms run
$125 to $200 a night. It is highly recommended.

NORTH TO MENDOCINO

Get an early start today to allow plenty of time for one of the most exciting days on your California journey. Your leisurely drive up the Redwood Highway leads through the picturesque Anderson Valley to the rugged Mendocino Coast. In any season this trip through Sonoma and Mendocino counties is a pleasure. The Golden Gate Bridge is the appropriate gateway to a mountainous region pocketed with handsome orchards, primeval redwood groves, and idyllic swimming holes like those of the Navarro River.

Suggested Schedule	
7:00 a.m.	Breakfast.
8:00 a.m.	Cross the Golden Gate Bridge and head north on Highway 101.
9:30 a.m.	Pause in Healdsburg for a snack or a dip in Russian River.
10:30 a.m.	Take S.R. 128 west in Cloverdale to Anderson Valley.
11:30 a.m.	Lunch in Boonville or Hendy Woods State Park, then proceed to Highway 1 north.
1:00 p.m.	Explore the town of Mendocino and check into your inn if you choose to stay here.
3:00 p.m.	Visit Russian Gulch State Park/Blowhole. Whale-watching in season.
4:00 p.m.	Visit Mendocino Coast Botanical Gardens.
5:00 p.m.	If you're staying in Fort Bragg, check into your motel or inn.
6:30 p.m.	Dinner in Mendocino or Fort Bragg, followed by sunset stroll and stargazing.

Country wineries will tempt you to pause for a bit of tasting. In spring, the coastal rhododendron fields will persuade nearly any traveler to slow down. In the fall, the vineyards of the Anderson Valley take on a golden aura as farmers serve fresh apple and cherry juice at their

roadside stands. And if you're looking for a first-class place
to dine or spend the night, this region has choices that will
delight nearly any tourist. Many restaurants also offer heav-
enly coastal views. Exploring this area gives you a feeling
of what California must have been like in an earlier time:
watching migrating whales, looking for purple urchins in
the tide pools, or seeing the tide surge into a blowhole at
Russian Gulch, you can visualize how the Mendocino coast
looked to its native residents, the Pomo Indians.

Travel Route: San Francisco to Mendocino (180 miles, 5 hours)

Leaving San Francisco, follow U.S. 101 north across the
Golden Gate Bridge through Marin and Sonoma counties.
About 90 minutes (68 miles) later, take the first Healdsburg
exit, which leads you directly to a Russian River waterfront
park perfect for a dip on a warm summer day. If you're
hungry, consider heading north on Healdsburg Avenue to
the Plaza, where you'll find the Downtown Fountain and
Bakery; partners include Lindsay Shere, who is also the pastry chef at one of California's best-known restaurants, Chez
Panisse. Closed Tuesday, (707) 431-2719. From here return
to U.S. 101 north. One mile north of Cloverdale you'll exit
west (left) on S.R. 128.

A serpentine route leads 27 miles west to Boonville, possibly the only city in America where English-speaking people need an interpreter. Although there is no phrase book
for "Boontling," the official language of Boonville, it's easy
to pick up some of the 1,000 words that comprise this
homespun vocabulary; a second language that has evolved
informally over several generations, this manner of speaking
is easily spotted. The pay phone is called "Buckey Walter,"
in honor of the man who installed the town's first telephone. And if you stop in at the Horn of Zeece Café ("cup
of coffee") you'll learn that pie here is called "Charlie
Brown." After lunch here or at a Navarro River picnic
ground in Hendy Woods State Park 10 miles farther west
on S.R. 128, proceed through a redwood forest to the
Mendocino coast where you'll head north (right) on
Highway 1.

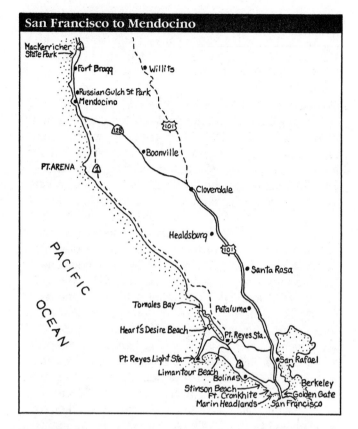

San Francisco to Mendocino

Mendocino

It's hard to believe that this lovely region, with its New England-style salt-box and Victorian homes, was a mariner's nightmare. Storm-lashed ships were washed into caves beneath the Mendocino bluffs and never seen again. Early settlers in the mid-nineteenth century were attracted by the prospect of salvaging cargo from major shipwrecks. Stop in at Mendocino's waterfront Jerome B. Ford House Visitor Center to orient yourself. You can pick up the Bear & Stebbins walking tour of local highlights such as the Kelley House Museum (open daily 1:00 p.m. to 4:00 p.m. June—October, Friday—Monday during the remainder of the year, [707] 937-5791), and the Mason temple crowned by a rooftop statue of Father Time and the Virgin, carved from a single piece of redwood. After exploring the town and headlands, fortify yourself with a Mendocino Ice Cream Company Black Forest cone, and head north (left) on Highway 1.

Sightseeing Highlights

▲▲▲**Russian Gulch State Park**—Located 2 miles north of Mendocino, this 1,245-acre preserve showcases many of the coastal region's distinguishing geographic features. Rugged headlands overlook the aquamarine sea. There are pine forests, a stream canyon leading back to waterfalls, and ridges thick with redwood, hemlock, and fir. Perhaps the most interesting geographic feature in the park is Devil's Punch Bowl, a 200-foot-long sea-cut tunnel adorned with wildflowers such as Douglas iris blooms, beach strawberries, ice plants, and the ubiquitous California poppy. The headland picnic area, with tables set in a grassy field overlooking prime skin diving and rock fishing, is one of the most picturesque places on the California coast. The only significant man-made structure is the bridge across Russian Gulch; its handsome parabolic arch makes a fine gateway for hikers headed upstream.

▲▲▲**Mendocino Coast Botanical Gardens**—Seven miles farther north on Highway 1 are the Mendocino Coast Botanical Gardens. In any season, you will enjoy strolling amidst the 10,000 plant varieties found in this 17-acre park. You can sit by the lily pond, explore Fern Canyon, or relax in the heather garden. Exotic and native trees are complemented by acres of rhododendrons, fuchsias, and azaleas. Digger Creek winds through pine forests to the coastal cliff house. The headlands are another excellent place to enjoy spring wildflowers. Admission is $5 for adults and $3 for youths ages 13 to 17. (707) 964-4352.

▲▲**Fort Bragg**—Leaving the garden you can make a left and continue north into Fort Bragg, or return south on Highway 1 to Mendocino. If you plan to take the Skunk Train redwood-country option tomorrow morning, consider staying at one of the many inns or motels available in Fort Bragg, a lumber town often overlooked by tourists in a hurry. The downtown district was one of the first five in California chosen to be part of a Main Street historic preservation project. Among the landmarks is Daly's department store on Highway 1, an all-redwood building that includes an upstairs art gallery. Next door at 343 North Main Street is the Guest House Museum, which tells the history of this lumber company town (open Wednesday—Sunday 10:00 a.m. to 4:00 p.m. April through October). The Fort building at 430 North Franklin is open Monday through Friday 9:00 a.m. to 5:00 p.m. Closed major holidays.

▲▲▲**Coast Walks**—Whether you spend the night in Fort Bragg or in Mendocino, be sure to consider taking a stroll after dinner. The Mendocino headlands are a delight at sunset. If you're staying in Fort Bragg, drive 3 miles north of town on Highway 1 to MacKerricher State Park. Park at Cleone Lake, a tidal lagoon with good rainbow trout fishing. From here it's a short walk to the old logging road that connects Pudding Creek near Fort Bragg to Ten Mile River at the north end of MacKerricher. The 7-mile section from Cleone Lake to Ten Mile River is closed to vehicular traffic. By foot or bike (rentals are available in Fort Bragg), any part of this coastline trail is a perfect way to end your day on the Mendocino coast.

Lodging

The Mendocino coast offers a wide variety of accommodations. Advance reservations are a good idea on weekends and during the summer and holiday periods. Prices in Fort Bragg tend to be lower than in Mendocino. You might want to base your decision on special interests; for instance, skin divers seeking out abalone and hikers interested in exploring the pygmy forest at Van Damme State Park may want to stay 3 miles south of Mendocino at the **Little River Inn**. This circa 1853 New England home with adjacent cottages offers a fine view of the coast. The restaurant is first-rate. Also on site are a nine-hole golf course and lighted tennis courts. Rooms and cottages run about $80 to $255. It's located at 7750 North Highway 1, Little River 95456. (707) 937-5942.

If you're eager to stay in the town of Mendocino, consider the **MácCallum House** at 45020 Albion Street, 95460. This Gothic revival house built in 1882 gives guests plenty of choices: antique-filled bedrooms in the main house or outbuildings that include a small cottage, greenhouse, converted barn, or even a water tower. The veranda is a perfect spot for lunch or a drink. After a long day there's no better way to unwind than to read or chat with other guests in front of the cobblestone fireplace. Rooms run about $75 to $180. (707) 937-0289.

Farther north in Fort Bragg, the **Noyo River Lodge**, at 500 Casa del Noyo Drive, 95437, has an ideal location above Noyo Harbor. This shingled bed and breakfast was built in 1868 and expanded half a century later to serve as the home of the local lumber mill superintendent. Shaded by cypress trees, the inn is enhanced by handcrafted board-and-batten interior paneling. At breakfast each morning you can watch the local fishing fleet head out into the ocean for salmon, cod, or snapper. To join the fun, hop aboard one of the Noyo Harbor party boats, where all tackle is provided. Or, if you prefer, simply walk down to the harbor to buy fresh or smoked fish. This is also a romantic dinner spot and a good place for a drink. Rooms run about $90 to $140. (707) 964-8045. Also recommended is **Seabird Lodge** at 191 South Street. (707) 964-4731. Rooms run $70 to $90.

A less expensive Fort Bragg alternative is **Tradewinds Lodge**, 400 S. Main Street, 95437. This standard motel offers rooms from about $59 to $105, depending on the season, a free shuttle to the Skunk Train, and an indoor pool. (707) 964-4761. Another possibility is the **Grey Whale Inn**, a bed and breakfast offering rooms for about $80 to $150. It's at 615 North Main Street, 95437. Phone (707) 964-0640 or (800) 382-7244. The **Colonial Inn** at 533 East Fir Street has comfortable rooms in a quiet location with some sea views. Rooms start around $60 (707) 964-9979. For additional lodging suggestions in various price categories, contact the Fort Bragg-Mendocino Coast Chamber of Commerce at P.O. Box 1141, Fort Bragg 95437. It's located on Main Street between Laurel and Redwood avenues; (707) 964-3153.

Excellent camping facilities along Highway 1 are available at **Van Damme State Park**, 3 miles south of Mendocino, **Russian Gulch State Park**, 2 miles north of Mendocino, and **MacKerricher State Park**, 3 miles north of Fort Bragg. To reserve space, call (800) 446-7275. For state park information, phone (707) 937-5804. Alternatively, try the **Mendocino Campground** at Highway 1 and Comptche-Ukiah Road, (707) 937-3130, or the **Woodside RV Park and Campground** at 17900 North Highway 1 in Fort Bragg, (707) 964-3684.

Food

Café Beaujolais, 961 Ukiah Street, is Mendocino's best-known breakfast spot. The waffles, pancakes, omelets, and crêpes here are all great. Lunches and dinners feature specialties like marinated sole, heaped with carrots, pine nuts, and currants, and poached salmon. Call (707) 937-5614 for reservations. Another good coastal view spot for breakfast is Mendocino's **Bay View Café** on the second level of 45040 Main Street. Brunch is served here on weekends, as are family "sunset" dinners. (707) 937-4197.

In Fort Bragg **Cap'n Flints**, at 32250 North Harbor Drive, is a fish-and-chips establishment popular with locals. Moderate prices and fast service make it a good choice for families. Nothing elegant, just fresh fish, chowder, and salads. Arrive early or expect to wait in line. (707) 964-9447. Another popular family spot is **D'Aurelio & Sons Pizza & Italian**, 438 Franklin. The homemade bread is first-rate. Come early on weekends. (707) 964-4227.

Itinerary Option

The Skunk Line in Fort Bragg offers three-hour trips to Northspur and an all-day trip to Willits. These trips are an excellent way to see the redwood country. Children love being able to stand outside on the excursion car to watch the Noyo River scenery. Originally a logging company railroad, the Skunk Line passes through majestic forests, fields of wildflowers, ranching country, and apple orchards. This is one of the best excursion rail rides in the West. The seven-hour round-trips operate year-round except Thanksgiving, Christmas, and New Year's Day. Half-day weekend trips operate daily from Fort Bragg and Willits from the third Saturday in June through the second Saturday in September. Additional half-day spring and fall service is available on Saturdays from Fort Bragg. Be sure to make reservations by calling (707) 964-6371.

AVENUE OF THE GIANTS

Just when you were wondering what could top Highway 1, today's journey takes you to the Avenue of the Giants. One of the state's most popular drives, this redwood country trip includes probably the best lumber mill tour in the American West, a visit to a company town, a Victorian village, and the north coast hub of Eureka.

Continuing north through Rockport, you'll rejoin Highway 101 at Leggett. This is the gateway to Humboldt County, reputed to be the marijuana-growing capital of California. The chances are slim that you will see any of the evil weed along your route. But you can count on uncrowded trails through the redwoods, herds of Roosevelt elk, warm river pools for swimming, good restaurants, museums, quaint inns, and little Victorian villages that retain their turn-of-the-century character. With its fine coastline, Humboldt County is also an ideal place for surf casting, rock hounding, or tide pooling. If you're willing to venture about 5 or 10 miles off the main highways, you won't have to worry about crowds in any season.

Suggested Schedule

7:30 a.m.	Breakfast.
8:30 a.m.	Visit Glass Beach in Fort Bragg.
9:00 a.m.	Take Highway 1 to U.S. 101 north.
11:00 a.m.	Drive through Avenue of the Giants.
12:00 noon	Lunch in the Redwoods.
2:30 p.m.	Tour Scotia Mill.
4:00 p.m.	Tour Ferndale.
5:30 p.m.	Arrive in Eureka, check into your hotel.
6:30 p.m.	Dinner.

Travel Route: Mendocino/Fort Bragg to Eureka (133 miles, 8 hours)

After leaving the Mendocino coast north of Rockport, Highway 1 heads inland on a twisty 17-mile route to

Leggett where you pick up U.S. 101 north to the 33-mile-long Avenue of the Giants. Your trip continues north through the redwood forests to Scotia. Thirteen miles farther north at Fernbridge, exit west (left) and continue 5 miles to Ferndale. From here, return to U.S. 101 north for the short trip to Eureka, a charming port town with hundreds of Victorian buildings.

Sightseeing Highlights

▲▲**Glass Beach**—One of the Mendocino coast's great secrets is Glass Beach at the north end of Fort Bragg. Glass from an old dump has been polished smooth by the pounding surf: the result is a cornucopia of brightly colored glass and pottery shards, eagerly scooped up by kids and adults alike. The beach is at the west end of Elm Street (any gas station can give you directions). Be sure to bring along buckets and shovels. As always, keep a close eye out for tides and rough surf. Children must remain with adults at all times.

▲▲▲**Avenue of the Giants**—Once spread across two million acres in California and Oregon, virgin redwoods are now found along a narrow 200,000-acre band extending from southern Oregon to Monterey County. You'll see some of the best-preserved groves as you travel the Avenue of the Giants, a route that parallels U.S. 101 for 33 miles. Between Sylvandale and Jordan Creek parks and side roads link up with 57,000 acres of park forestland. Expect to spend a lot of time looking skyward as you make your way north: the world's tallest tree, the redwood rises as high as 300 feet. Some of the virgin forest you'll see includes trees that date back to the birth of Christ. Much of this primeval treasure has been lost due to the strong market for redwood, a most durable forest product. As you travel through these forests, give thanks to the foresight of preservationist forces like the Save the Redwoods League who have turned these virgin groves into prize parkland. (Incidentally, you'll be doubling back on this route in a couple of days; this will give you a chance to spend additional time exploring these handsome parks.)

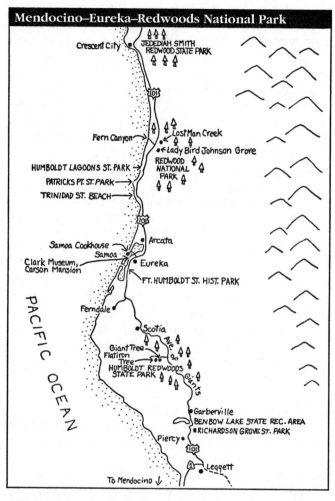

Mendocino–Eureka–Redwoods National Park

Crescent City

JEDEDIAH SMITH
REDWOOD STATE PARK

Lost Man Creek

Fern Canyon →

←Lady Bird Johnson Grove

HUMBOLDT LAGOONS ST. PARK →

REDWOOD
NATIONAL
PARK

PATRICKS PT. ST. PARK →

TRINIDAD ST. BEACH →

Arcata

Samoa Cookhouse →
Samoa

Clark Museum,
Carson Mansion

Eureka

FT. HUMBOLDT ST. HIST. PARK

PACIFIC OCEAN

Ferndale

Scotia

Giant Tree
Flatiron
Tree
HUMBOLDT REDWOODS
STATE PARK

Ave. of the Giants

Garberville
BENBOW LAKE STATE REC. AREA
■RICHARDSON GROVE ST. PARK

Piercy

Leggett

To Mendocino ↓

▲▲**Richardson Grove**—Located on U.S. 101 9 miles south of Garberville, this park is a delightful sanctuary adjacent to the Eel River where you may want to go for a swim during the warm summer months. Excellent scenic walks include the 1.3-mile Lookout Trail and the 2-mile Toumey Trail. Winter silver and king salmon and steelhead make the park popular with fishermen. (707) 247-3378.

▲**Shrine Redwood Tree**—13078 Avenue of the Giants, Myers Flat. Generations of California tourists have pho-

tographed their cars driving through a redwood tree:
here's your chance to join them. You can also pick up
redwood burl souvenirs here. Made from stumpage,
they are produced by independent artisans in the area.

▲▲**Rockefeller Forest**—Eight miles north of the
Shrine Tree, turn left on Bull Creek Flat Road for the 5-
mile trip west to the Rockefeller Forest. This grove is
one of redwood country's chosen spots. It's also an
excellent place to stop for a picnic lunch.

▲▲▲**Scotia**—Scotia is a handsome company town
with cradle-to-grave security for workers and their families. The north coast was colonized by many communities like this, but Scotia is the only one that perpetuates
the paternalistic system. With its 300 well-kept redwood
homes, a medical center, bank, schools, and shops,
little Scotia looks like a good place to live. A typical
two-bedroom home rents for $200 a month. Every high
school graduate here who enters a four-year college
program can count on an $8,000 scholarship. There
have been no significant layoffs here since the
Depression. Retirees have to give up their houses and
move, but they can always come back and stay at the
first-class Scotia Inn, a hotel and restaurant popular
with tourists.

A short drive north of the Avenue of the Giants,
Scotia is reached by exiting west off U.S. 101 onto Main
Street. Head for the museum where you'll get a pass for
the self-guided Pacific Lumber Mill tour, an excellent
nour-long overview of this redwood operation from
debarking to finishing. It's open Monday through Friday
8:00 a.m. to 10:30 a.m. and noon to 2:30 p.m. Closed
holidays, the week of July 4, and Christmas. (707) 764-
2222. The province of the Pacific Lumber Company, this
mill has traditionally enjoyed a good reputation with
environmentalists and has been cooperative about selling off lands to create some of the redwood parks you
just visited. Several years ago the firm was sold and
new owners began stepping up redwood logging. The
company backed off this aggressive cutting program
after protests from a number of environmental groups.

▲▲▲**Ferndale**—Continue north on U.S. 101 to Fernbridge where you exit west (left). Continue 5 miles
through dairy country and across the Salt River to
Ferndale, another fascinating little Humboldt County
community. A few years back the State Department of
Parks and Recreation came here to designate some of the
town's architectural landmarks. But after thinking the
matter over, officials gave up and simply decided to
declare the whole town a State Historic Landmark. As
soon as you arrive you'll see why. Even an earthquake in
spring 1992 was not enough to alter Ferndale's charm.
The streets here are lined with butterfat palaces built by
wealthy dairy farmers; they have names like the Skim
Milk and Gum Drop Tree houses. Main Street remains in
its full nineteenth-century glory thanks to a local rancher,
Viola Russ McBride. This third-generation resident took it
upon herself to buy up all the landmark buildings in the
early 1960s before new owners could tamper with their
handsome features. Today, when she comes down from
her ranch, Ms. McBride can visit a delightful array of
shops that will satisfy nearly any taste or palate. Tourists
share her enthusiasm. If you've had it with fast food,
consider Becker's Pool Hall, a lunch counter that still displays an old signboard featuring crab sandwiches for 15
cents. The locals leave their shotguns on the table next to
the dining area. In the rear, dairy farmers play their daily
game of cards on tables beneath hooded lamps dangling
from the high ceiling.

While in this Victorian village you'll also want to
browse at a number of Main Street establishments such
as Golden Gait Mercantile, an old-fashioned emporium
that is filled with patent medicines and collectibles like
Bing Crosby ice cream cartons. A few doors away is
kinetic metal sculptor Stan Bennett, best known for his
magic marble machines. Bennett's shop is always a big
hit with children. Nearby is Ferndale Books, a good place
to shop for Californiana. It's run by Carlos Benemann
and his wife, Marilyn. (Carlos won this store in a poker
game.) Even if you're not planning to spend a night here,
be sure to walk two blocks east of Main Street to 400

Berding Street. Here you'll find the Gingerbread Mansion Bed and Breakfast, a creamsicle-colored Victorian house landscaped with formal English gardens.

After visiting the town museum at Third and Shaw streets and picking up a handmade Humboldt County Goo Goo Bar (made with full cream caramels) at Sweetness and Light on Main Street, it's time to return to U.S. 101 and drive north (left) to Humboldt Bay.

▲▲**Eureka**—The fleet here catches much of the fresh fish served in Bay Area restaurants. As you might expect in a town with 1,600 homes of historic importance, Eureka has the state's best-known Victorian building, the three-story Carson Mansion that currently serves as a private club. Built of redwood, mahogany, and primavera, this spinach-colored masterpiece is at the north end of the city's newly refurbished Old Town district. To reach this landmark just take U.S. 101 through downtown Eureka to M Street. Turn left and drive two blocks to Second Street. Although visitors are not allowed inside, you can take some memorable exterior photos.

After visiting the mansion you may want to take a left on Second Street and stroll down into Old Town. Among the bed and breakfasts, restaurants, offices, and shops here is Romano Gabriel's wooden sculpture garden. A kind of Watts Towers of the North, this folk art monument was moved here after Gabriel's death in 1977. Carved entirely from vegetable crates, the collection includes sprays of flowers, Italian salami, and a vast smattering of humanity arranged shooting-gallery style. This whimsical collage is a very special piece of folk art and an appropriate end to your day's journey.

Lodging

Eureka offers a wide range of accommodations ranging from elegant inns to inexpensive motels. Located in a restored two-story Victorian, **Hotel Carter** at 301 L Street, Eureka 95501, is a new establishment with an old-fashioned touch. It's affiliated with the **Carter House Bed and Breakfast Inn** across the street at 1033 Third Street. The antique-furnished hotel is comfortably appointed with a handsome lobby where you have continental breakfast and afternoon wine and cheese. The Hotel Carter is conveniently located in the Old Town area, just a few blocks from the Carson Mansion. About $115 to $225. (707) 445-1390. Our budget choice in town is the **Fort Humboldt Motel**, 1503 McCullens Avenue, Eureka 95501. Rooms run $35 to $50. (707) 442-0222.

If you fell in love with Ferndale, half an hour south of Eureka, spend the night at **The Gingerbread Mansion**, 400 Berding Street. This elegant Victorian is one of the finest bed and breakfasts in Humboldt County. (Rooms here even come with two matching clawfoot bathtubs.) Free bicycles are available for touring. Be sure to try the Very Lemony Lemon Bread, which won first prize in the quickbread category at a statewide B&B competition (judges included Julia Child). About $85 to $185. (707) 786-4000.

Another possibility 7 miles north of Eureka is the **Lady Anne Bed and Breakfast**. It's located at 902 14th Street, Arcata 95521. Rooms in this Queen Anne start at about $60 with shared bath. (707) 822-2797. In the summer months, the **Arcata Crew House Hostel** offers lodging for $10 at 1390 I Street, Arcata 95521. (707) 822-9995.

Campers: KOA Eureka, 4050 N. Hwy 101, Eureka 95501. Located 4 miles north of Eureka, near Arcata Bay, this trailer park/campground is central to the region's main attractions. Rates are $20 to $23. (707) 822-4243. The nearest public campgrounds are in the Trinidad area about 20 miles north. For details, see Day 19.

Food

For atmosphere, it's hard to beat the **Samoa Cookhouse** on Cookhouse Lane in Samoa. This venerable establishment serves the same kind of authentic lumberjack cuisine it once prepared daily for 500. With its red-checked tablecloths, homemade bread, and small museum, this red clapboard establishment delights tourists. Heaping bowls of vegetables and platters of chicken, ham, or beef are served family-style. Fruit pies are served for dessert, but don't bother asking for a slice: waitresses will only serve an entire pie hot from the oven; it's all included in the tab, which runs about $10 for adults, less for children. This all-you-can-eat approach is a bargain that draws long lines, but don't expect gourmet fare. To avoid waiting, arrive early. Breakfasts are a good bet here. (707) 442-1659. Take U.S. 101 north to S.R. 255, turn left and drive over the bridge to the Samoa Peninsula, where signs will guide you to the restaurant.

Seafood is a must here. I'm partial to **Jonah's SeaFood Grotto and Market**, 665 Samoa Boulevard, Arcata. This moderately priced establishment is located about fifteen minutes north of Eureka. The drive is worth it. A market here retails the same fresh salmon, Dungeness crab, halibut, and snapper you can order for dinner. Recommended for seafood lovers. (707) 822-5996. In Eureka, another popular spot for fresh fish is the **Seafood Grotto**, 605 Broadway. (707) 443-2075.

One of the better Italian restaurants in Eureka is **Roy's**, 218 D Street. (707) 442-4574.

Helpful Hint
The Eureka-Humboldt County Convention and Visitors Bureau is at 1034 Second Street, Eureka 95501. (707) 443-5097 or (800) 346-3482. In California, (800) 338-7352.

EUREKA TO TRINIDAD

After a look at Eureka's most important museum, drive north to the seacoast town of Trinidad and the redwood parks. You'll have a chance to enjoy several of the region's best short hikes, see wildlife, and beachcomb at your leisure. In the process, you'll sample some of northern California's best-kept secrets—idyllic spots that most visitors speed right by. Don't forget to bring extra film.

Suggested Schedule	
8:30 a.m.	Breakfast at the Samoa Cookhouse or your inn.
10:00 a.m.	Visit Eureka's Clarke Museum.
11:00 a.m.	Drive north on U.S. 101 to Redwood National Park.
12:00 noon	Stop at Park Visitor's Center in Orick.
12:30 p.m.	Picnic at Lady Bird Johnson Grove.
2:00 p.m.	Visit Roosevelt Elk Preserve, Fern Canyon, and Gold Bluff Beach in Prairie Creek Redwoods State Park.
4:00 p.m.	Return to Redwood National Park and hike Lost Man Creek Trail.
5:00 p.m.	Drive back to Trinidad for dinner. Overnight here or at Eureka/Arcata.

Travel Route: Eureka to Redwood National Park (125 miles round-trip)

From Eureka, take U.S. 101 north to Redwood National Park Visitor Center at Orick. Continue north to Bald Hills Road and turn right (east) to the Lady Bird Johnson Grove. Returning to U.S. 101, head north to Davidson Road where you turn left, and continue 8 miles on a dirt road (restrictions apply, see below) to Gold Bluff Beach in Prairie Creek Redwoods State Park. Return to U.S. 101, head north about one mile to the Lost Man Creek turnoff. After parking and hiking this easy 1.5-mile round-trip to the cascade on Lost Man Creek, return south on U.S. 101 to Trinidad and Eureka/Arcata.

Sightseeing Highlights

▲▲**Clarke Museum**—Located at Third and E streets in Eureka is an excellent collection built around the region's Native American, maritime, and lumber history. The former Bank of Eureka building is an impressive home for this museum that has over 1,200 examples of Yurok, Karuk, Hupa, and Wiyot Indian basketry. Used as dishes and cookware, storage vessels, and baby carriers, these traditional baskets are handsome examples of Native American handicraft. Wandering amidst the Roman-Renaissance revival building's high arches and pilasters, illuminated by a stained-glass skylight, is a fine way to begin your day on the north coast. Notable exhibits include antique weapons, Victorian furnishings, toys, and dolls. The museum is open Tuesday through Saturday noon to 4:00 p.m. Closed on holidays and in January. (707) 443-1947. Donations accepted.

▲▲**Redwood National Park**—Located about an hour north of Eureka via U.S. 101, this 78,000-acre refuge is the state's newest national park. After passing first-class state parks at Patrick's Point and Humboldt Lagoons, you'll reach the Visitor Center at Orick. This is a good place to acquaint yourself with the many splendors of Redwood National Park. A shuttle bus from the Visitor Center can take you to the Tall Trees trailhead in the summer months. The strenuous 4-mile loop descends 800 feet into the grove, where you'll find some of the world's highest trees. While this four- to five-hour trip is worthwhile, our plan today calls for a short drive north from Orick on U.S. 101 to Bald Hills Road. Turn right here to reach the Lady Bird Johnson Grove. The half-hour-long nature trail here is an excellent way to see some of the great redwoods. It's particularly fine in the springtime when the purple rhododendron, red clintonia, and white trillium bloom in abundance. Be sure to pick up the self-guided brochure at the trailhead. For more information on the park, call (707) 488-3461.

▲▲**Prairie Creek Redwoods State Park**—A 10-mile drive on Davidson Road west of U.S. 101 (vehicles over 7 feet by 20 feet are prohibited, use caution in wet winter weather) takes you to Gold Bluff Beach. Although the prospectors who flocked here in the mid-nineteenth century struck out, modern visitors are seldom disappointed. Camping is popular in the remote dunes, which are home to an impressive herd of Roosevelt elk. A mile farther on, the road dead-ends near the entrance to Fern Canyon. This 0.7-mile walk along Home Creek takes you into a coastal Eden where small waterfalls trickle down canyon walls covered with sword ferns, lady ferns, and five-fingered ferns. For more information, call (707) 488-2171.

▲▲▲**Lost Man Creek**—Fern Canyon is one dimension of primeval California. For another, retrace your trip on Davidson Road to U.S. 101 and head north a short distance to Lost Man Creek. Turn right and you'll soon be at the trailhead for one of Redwood Country's best short hikes. Although it's only a few minutes from the highway, expect plenty of privacy as you take this easy 1.5-mile round-trip along a redwood-lined stream. Bridges along the way create ideal vantage points for photographing the cascading creek. Don't miss this delightful forest walk.

▲▲**Trinidad**—When you're ready to return to civilization, head south on U.S. 101 to this coastal seaport—our dinner choice tonight. After you've explored the coast at Trinidad Head, a promontory that can easily be circled via a footpath, it's time for dinner at the Seascape, where you can enjoy the sunset over the harbor. Afterward, check in at one of the local inns or campgrounds. If you prefer, return to Eureka/Arcata and last night's lodging.

Lodging
If you'd like to spend the night in a Cape Cod-style inn with a panoramic view of Trinidad Bay, try the **Trinidad Bed and Breakfast** at 560 Edwards Street, 95570. This inn is within walking distance of Trinidad's many attractions, including beachcombing and fishing. Rates run about $90 to $155. (707) 677-0840. A number of budget motels are located just north of town. Among them is the **Patrick's Point Inn**, 3602 Patrick's Point Drive, Trinidad

95570. It's near the sea and Patrick's Point State Park.
Close to sea lion habitat. Rooms start around $40. Phone
(707) 677-3483. Also try **Lost Whale Bed and Breakfast**,
3452 Patrick's Point Drive. Rates start at about $90.
(707) 677-3425.

Campers: Your best bet is **Patrick's Point State
Park**. Exit west from U.S. 101 5 miles north of Trinidad.
This is one of the finest coastal parks in redwood country. You'll enjoy the hike along forested bluffs where it's
possible to spot sea lions, harbor seals, and, in season,
migrating whales. Be sure to climb down to Agate Beach
where jade abounds. Birders should not miss this park;
it's a fine place to spot cormorants, gulls, and numerous
songbirds. A small natural history and Indian museum is
also of interest. (707) 677-3570. If the park is full, try the
View Crest Lodge Campground at 3415 Patrick's Point
Drive, Trinidad. (707) 677-3393.

Food

The best place to watch the sunset in Trinidad is the
Seascape, (707) 677-3762. Since it's located on the town
pier, you know the fish is fresh; good omelets for breakfast. Incidentally, if you're wondering what all those
swank cars are doing in the parking lot at **Larrupin
Café**, 1658 Patrick's Point Drive, Trinidad, why not make
a dinner reservation? The locals believe the continental
dining here is among the region's best. A lot of tourists
agree. Call (707) 677-0230 as seating is limited.

Itinerary Options

Azalea State Reserve: Located above the Mad River 5
miles north of Arcata, this hillside park is a winner in the
late spring and early summer when it is pretty in pink
blossoms. Take U.S. 101 north to S.R. 200 and exit right
(east) to the park. Open daytime only. (707) 445-6547.

Del Norte County: If you want to continue north to
the Oregon border, drive north on U.S. 101 after finishing
your hike at Lost Man Creek. After entering Del Norte
County you'll soon reach Klamath, a good headquarters
for steelhead fishing, rafting, and jet-boat tours on the

Klamath River. Del Norte County has a number of fine redwood state parks, including Jedediah Smith State Park where you'll find eighteen memorial redwood groves, fishing, and sandy bathing beaches on the Smith River. (707) 464-9533. Del Norte Coast Redwoods State Park is a good place to visit in the spring when the azaleas and rhododendrons are in bloom or in the fall when the alder leaves turn. (707) 464-9533. In Crescent City, you may want to stop for information at the Redwood National Park Headquarters at 1111 Second Street, (707) 464-6101. North of town you can explore a region that produces 90 percent of the nation's lily bulbs. Growers here sponsor an "Easter in July" Festival.

Tempted to step over the Oregon border? The remaining half of coastal U.S. 101 is covered in *2 to 22 Days in the Pacific Northwest.* Author Richard Harris picks up just across the state line at Gold Beach and continues north along one of the west's most scenic routes.

EUREKA TO SONOMA

Today's drive takes you south along the Eel River to
Mendocino County and the Valley of the Moon. After
passing back through the redwood parks, you'll be able
to visit a Tudor mansion, pause for a dip at your choice
of lakes or streams, and perhaps take time out to visit a
winery or two. Your day ends in Sonoma, a community
that has done a splendid job of preserving its political,
religious, and literary history.

Suggested Schedule

7:30 a.m.	Breakfast.
8:30 a.m.	Leave Eureka on U.S. 101 south.
9:30 a.m.	Visit Benbow Inn and Benbow Lake.
12:00 noon	Lunch in Willits.
3:00 p.m.	Visit Jack London State Historic Park.
5:30 p.m.	Check into your Sonoma hotel.

Travel Route: Eureka to Sonoma (250 miles)
You'll be on U.S. 101 south for most of today's journey.
Take S.R. 12 south from Santa Rosa until you reach
Arnold Drive. Turn right (west) here and proceed into
Glen Ellen. Signs will lead you to Jack London State
Historic Park via London Ranch Road. After you leave the
park, take Arnold Drive south to Petaluma Avenue. Turn
left (east) here. Petaluma Avenue turns into West Napa
Street, which takes you to the Sonoma Plaza.

Sightseeing Highlights
▲▲**Redwood Parks**—Rick Steves, who originated the
22 Days itinerary planner series, doesn't despair about
missing sites on a trip. He takes the Douglas McArthur
approach to travel: "I shall return." You will, too, and
here's the proof: if you wanted to spend more time in
those memorable redwood parks you visited on Day 18,
do it now.

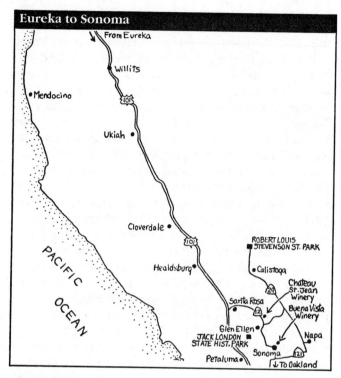

▲▲Benbow Lake State Park—An ideal place to stop
for a swim on a warm summer day. Paddleboats rented
here are also fun. Just across the way is the Tudor-style
Benbow Inn. Now in its sixth decade, this establishment
has served famous visitors like Herbert Hoover, Eleanor
Roosevelt, and Charles Laughton. Anglophiles will love
the formal dining. Incidentally, if you're feeling really laid
back and have some extra time, you may want to stay 6
miles south on U.S. 101 at the Hartsook Inn in Piercy. It
offers modest cottages convenient to Eel River swimming
holes. (Ask for a room away from the highway.) Kids
love this one. You're next door to Richardson Grove
State Park. Call (707) 946-2311.

▲▲▲Jack London State Park—Biographer W. A.
Swanberg once wrote that Hollywood was divided into
two castes: those who had been invited to San Simeon
and those who had not. While celebrities came by the

trainload to Hearst's castle, Jack London was more selective about the guests he invited to his ranch in the Valley of the Moon. Convinced that "if we redeem the land, it will redeem us," London was an early-day organic farmer who followed the soil conservation, terracing, and crop rotation principles of his Santa Rosa neighbor, Luther Burbank. London proudly showed visitors the state's first hollow-block silo and a "Pig Palace" that gave each sow and her brood a private apartment and sun porch. Also on his tour were the cooperage, winery, blacksmith shop, and well-maintained manure pit.

The original 130-acre ranch where London lived from 1911 to 1916 is now partly owned by his grandnephew, Milo Shepherd. The remaining 803 ranch acres are preserved by the state as Jack London State Park in the Valley of the Moon. Spared development, this woodsy retreat looks much the way it did in London's day. It's open from 8:00 a.m. to sunset. Near the entrance is a museum located in the House of Happy Walls (open 10:00 a.m. to 5:00 p.m.), which the writer's widow, Charmian, built as a memorial in 1919. Here you'll find London's old office, manuscripts, brass bed, and South Seas collection gathered during a 27-month honeymoon trip on his 42-foot ketch, the *Snark*. If you've never read his autobiographical novel *Martin Eden*, pick up a paperback copy in the gift shop. Every writer and would-be writer will appreciate this story of London's rite of passage. By the way, the Jack London Bookstore at 14300 Arnold Drive in Glen Ellen probably has the widest selection of London literature to be found anywhere. Phone (707) 996-2888.

A pleasant half-mile walk from the museum is the site of the Londons' dream domicile, the Wolf House. The Socialist spared no expense on this 26-room mansion with nine fireplaces, a library, stag party room, gun and trophy room, courtyard, a reflecting pool, and a fireproof vault for manuscripts. Draft horses hauled in big boulders of volcanic lava that were framed with steel and redwood to erect the Wolf House. On August 22, 1913, just before the Londons planned to vacate their nearby cottage and move into the house, a fire consumed the Wolf House, leaving only the stone foundation, walls, and chimney. After exploring the ruins, retrace your steps and walk over to the ranch where you can see London's farm buildings and the cottage where he wrote many of his stories. A 9-mile network of hiking trails is available should you care to return for a longer visit tomorrow. The Sonoma Cattle Company runs guided horseback rides up a 2-mile trail to the Sonoma Mountain summit. Reserve by calling (707) 996-8566. The best time to visit here is fall when vineyard leaves are turning and the park looks like an impressionist painting.

Although London's career was cut short in 1916, when he died of uremic poisoning at the age of forty, he left an extensive legacy. Besides his fifty books—which have been translated into thirty languages—he wrote hundreds of short stories that are standard reading in literature classes throughout the world. He once wrote, "I would rather be a superb meteor, every atom of me in magnificent glow, than a sleepy and permanent planet. The proper function of man is to live, not to exist. I shall not waste my days in trying to prolong them. I shall use my time."

Lodging

My favorite Sonoma Valley B&B is **Morningsong** at 21725 Hyde Road. (707) 939-8616. Rooms starting at $60 open onto a pear orchard. The breakfasts are terrific. A great location and a great value.

If you are looking for a rural experience, consider the **Beltane Ranch Bed and Breakfast.** It's located at 11775 Sonoma Highway (Highway 12), Glen Ellen 95442. On a slope of the Mayacama Range, the 1892 Beltane Ranch House (once a bordello) offers a fine view of the Sonoma Valley vineyards. Children are allowed by arrangement. About $95 to $140. (707) 996-6501.

In Sonoma the **El Dorado Hotel** at 405 West First Street is an excellent choice. $80 to $140. (707) 996-3030. The **Sonoma Hotel** at 110 West Spain Street is furnished with an eclectic blend of Spanish, Italian, Austrian, and American heirlooms. Maya Angelou wrote *Gather*

Together in My Name in room 21 on the third floor.
About $75 to $125. (707) 996-2996. Another conveniently
located establishment on the square is the **Thistle Dew
Inn** at 171 West Spain Street, 95476. It consists of a pair
of homes decorated with arts-and-crafts California furniture circa 1910. Complimentary bicycle rentals. About
$100 to $135. Call (707) 938-2909. Our budget choice is
the **Jack London Lodge** in nearby Glen Ellen at 13740
Arnold Drive. Rates run $55 to $75. (707) 938-8510.

The elite flock to the **Sonoma Mission Inn & Spa**
Boyes Boulevard and Highway 12, 95476. Rooms run
$165 to $325. Discounts apply during the winter months.
(707) 938-9000. Up the valley in Kenwood is the charming **Kenwood Inn & Spa** bed and breakfast at 10400
Highway 12. $165 to $275. (707) 833-1293.

Campers: Try **Sugarloaf Ridge State Park**, 2605
Adobe Canyon Road, Kenwood. Camping here is $14 per
night. RVs up to 24 feet are welcome. Reserve by calling
(800) 444-7275. If Sugarloaf is full, try **Spring Lake
Regional Park** off Montgomery or Summerfield Drive,
Santa Rosa. (707) 539-8082. Camping is $9 per night on
a first-come, first-served basis.

Food

For good country cuisine, try the **Kenwood Restaurant
and Bar**, 9900 Highway 12, Kenwood. (707) 833-6326.
On the Sonoma Plaza, the historic **Swiss Hotel**, 18 West
Spain Street, has fine patio dining. (707) 938-2884. For
excellent seafood, try the expensive **Eastside Oyster Bar**
at 133 East Napa Street. (707) 939-1266. I also recommend **Rin's Thai Restaurant** at 599 Broadway, (707)
938-8788, and the excellent sandwiches and salads at
Feed Store Cafe, 529 First Street West. (707) 938-2122
For deli or takeout fare, head for the **Sonoma Cheese
Factory and Delicatessen**, 2 Spain Street. You're welcome to watch the cheese-making. (707) 996-1000.

An excellent dinner choice is **Bistro Lunel** at 110 W.
Spain Street. (707) 939-1889. The patio is a perfect place to
enjoy lunch, dinner, or Sunday brunch. There's also a great
bar here.

SONOMA

Today you'll take a leisurely walk through historic Sonoma, learn about great moments in California history, and visit the state's oldest operating premium winery. Your hub is the Sonoma Plaza, a handsome park surrounded by the state's northernmost mission, adobes built in the Mexican period, territorial buildings, office blocks created by Italian craftsmen, and, of course, the fine shops that will provide the loaf of bread and jug of wine for today's picnic lunch here.

Suggested Schedule

9:00 a.m.	Breakfast.
10:00 a.m.	Begin Sonoma Walking Tour.
12:00 noon	Lunch in the Sonoma Plaza.
1:00 p.m.	Resume Walking Tour.
2:00 p.m.	Visit Buena Vista Winery.
3:00 p.m.	Bike, ride, swim, or see another winery.
6:00 p.m.	Dinner in Sonoma.

Travel Route

Today's walking tour is summarized in a brochure put out by the Sonoma League for Historic Preservation. It's available at the **Sonoma Valley Visitors Bureau** located in the old Carnegie Library on the Plaza at 453 First Street East. (707) 996-1090. While here you can also pick up information on the region's wineries, parks, restaurants, and recreational opportunities. (Incidentally, all the purveyors you'll need to supply your picnic lunch are located here on the plaza.)

Sonoma

When the Spaniards first arrived in this handsome coastal valley, it was a hunting and gathering ground favored by the Pomo and Coastal Miwok Indian tribes. In 1823, the Indians were baptized by Mission Padre José Altamira and put to work for Mexico. An Indian uprising in 1826

partially burned the mission and forced Father Altamira
to flee. Then, in 1834, General Mariano Guadalupe
Vallejo was sent to secularize the mission. But three years
after they were freed from the mission, the Indians were
decimated by a smallpox epidemic. Vallejo laid out the
town around an eight-acre plaza and built barracks for
his troops and a fine adobe, La Casa Grande, for himself.
As immigrants began arriving in this fertile valley, the resident Mexican general began advocating annexation of
California by the United States. In June 1846, Vallejo was
arrested by the Bear Flag party, which took the city on
behalf of the independent Republic of California. One
month after the nonviolent revolt, American naval forces
took Monterey, raised the Stars and Stripes, and declared
the republic United States territory. In 1848, after the
Mexican government signed the Treaty of Guadalupe
Hidalgo with the United States, Vallejo turned to wine
making, served two terms as mayor of Sonoma, and
eventually became the region's first state senator. Fortunately, thanks to the city's rural tradition and—until

recently—slow growth, its historic resources have been well preserved. Today's itinerary allows you to walk through this historic drama and provides an excellent overview of the transition from Indian times through Mexican dominion to the present day.

Sightseeing Highlights
▲▲▲Mission San Francisco Solano—The last of California's twenty-one missions, this landmark has been handsomely restored. Here you'll see the rebuilt 1823 chapel distinguished by its pulpit and wall paintings. The hand-hewn timbers are tied together with leather thongs and the original earthen floor has been bricked and tiled. A small museum tells the story of the community's evolution from mission town to military outpost to wine-making hub. On display here are sixty-two mission watercolors by artist Chris Jorgensen. Archaeologists have recently uncovered remnants of the padres' quarters, tile walk-ways, and sacristy. Be sure to visit the courtyard, where you'll see working replicas of the beehive ovens used to bake mission bread. Open daily 10:00 a.m. to 5:00 p.m. Admission is $2 for adults and $1 for children.
▲The Barracks—This two-story adobe at First Street East and East Spain Street was built by Indians for the Mexican troops. More than 100 military expeditions set out from this point to subdue local Indian tribes; many of these expeditions were led by Vallejo. After the Bear Flag takeover, the barracks became home for the Bear Flag followers. Subsequently, the barracks were taken over by American military forces who established a major outpost. In 1860, Vallejo turned the building into a winery. The barracks subsequently served as a print shop, store, and private home before the state bought the structure and restored it in recent years. Open daily 10:00 a.m. to 5:00 p.m.
▲Toscano Hotel—At 20 East Spain Street, this is an early California-style frame building. The overhanging second-story balcony features Greek revival detailing. Tours include a look at the turn-of-the-century kitchen and dining room.

▲**La Casa Grande Servants Quarters**—At 20 East Spain Street this is the site of General Vallejo's first home. Finished in 1840, the big house was the birthplace of all eleven Vallejo children. A diplomatic and social hub of the region, this home gained a three-story adobe tower in 1843. General Vallejo, his brother, and brother-in-law were arrested here by the Bear Flag party in June 1846. The main wing of the house was destroyed by fire in 1867, leaving only the two-story adobe servants' wing standing today.

▲**First Baptist Church**—At 542 First Street East, this is a handsome Gothic revival with a Christopher Wren-style steeple. Note the square belfry with louvered gabled vents, octagonal tower, and metal finial weather vane.

▲▲**Clewe House**—This superb Italianate mansion at 531 Second Street East on Nathanson Creek features two flat-roof verandas with decorated capitals and brackets. Note the mansard overhanging roofs, paneled frieze boards and wrought-iron roof cresting. Across the street is the Duhring House, a handsome Colonial revival.

▲▲▲**Vallejo Home** is reached by taking Spain Street west to Third Street and turning right about a half-mile from the plaza. The entrance is a quarter-mile-long drive-way lined with cottonwood trees and Castilian roses. The home was done in the Carpenter Gothic style popular on the Atlantic seaboard. Insulated by bricks placed inside the walls, each room had its own white marble fireplace. Among the fine furnishings were crystal chandeliers, lace curtains, and a rosewood concert grand piano. Vallejo and his wife lived here for thirty-five years. Late in life they were forced to sell most of his vast holdings—including his prized vineyard—due to a series of economic setbacks. Today the house is a state-run museum furnished with many of the Vallejo family's personal effects. Open daily 10:00 a.m. to 5:00 p.m.

▲**Vasquez House**—This gabled home located off First Street East in the El Paseo complex is headquarters for the Sonoma League for Historic Preservation, which has mapped out the walking tour you are now taking. The shop and library here are good places to learn more about the history of the region. Open Wednesday through Sunday 1:00 p.m. to 5:00 p.m.

▲▲**Buena Vista Winery**—The state's oldest premium winery is a short drive east of town, at 18000 Old Winery Road, Sonoma. From the plaza, take East Napa Street to Old Winery Road and turn left. Located in a eucalyptus glen, the winery offers tasting in an 1862 press house/art gallery. From the outside you can view the cellars built here in 1857 by Count Agoston Haraszathy, a Hungarian exile. The pioneer vintner, who brought vineyard cuttings from Europe, persuaded many wine makers to leave the old country for California. A fine place for a picnic, the grounds are also a popular location for classical concerts, dramas, and other special events during the summer months. Open daily 10:00 a.m. to 5:00 p.m. (707) 938-1266. Next door to the winery is the new **Bartholomew Memorial Park**. It features a re-creation of Agoston Haraszthy's original villa. It's open Wednesdays, Saturdays and Sundays. Don't miss this one. You must call for reservations. (707) 938-2244.

▲**Chateau St. Jean**—This premium winery located at 8555 Sonoma Highway, Kenwood, has a self-guided tour. The winery's white wines enjoy an excellent reputation. It's located 10 miles north of Sonoma on S.R. 12. Open daily 10:30 a.m. to 5:00 p.m. (707) 833-4134.

Food
Everything you need for the picnic lunch can be bought from shops clustered around the plaza. The **Sonoma Cheese Factory** is at 2 West Spain Street. For bread, visit the **Sonoma French Bakery** at 468 First Street East, open Tuesday through Saturday 7:30 a.m. to 5:00 p.m. and Sunday 7:30 a.m. to 4 p.m. For dessert, try the **Old Sonoma Creamery** at 400 First Street East.

Optional Extension: Napa Valley
The neighboring Napa Valley is a short drive from Sonoma. You can drive direct to Napa via S.R. 12/121 or take Trinity Road, Dry Creek Road, and Oakville Road east from S.R. 12 at Glen Ellen. Either way you'll have a

chance to visit some of the state's best-known wineries, hot springs resorts, and the region immortalized by Robert Louis Stevenson in his book, *Silverado Squatters.* It was here in spring 1880 that the writer, broke and seriously ill with tuberculosis, honeymooned with his new bride, Fanny Osbourne (his courtship in Monterey paid off). The couple and her 12-year-old son by a previous marriage moved into the abandoned bunkhouse of the old Silverado Mine. Not only did the writer regain his health here on the mountain but he also won parental acceptance of his marriage and an annual allowance that let him resume his writing career.

Although Stevenson's stay in the Napa Valley was relatively brief, it had an important impact on his subsequent work. Descriptions of the region abound in his writing. "Juan Silverado," a Mexican slang description of the mine where he stayed, is believed to have inspired the name Long John Silver.

Today you can hike to the honeymoon cabin in Robert Louis Stevenson State Park on S.R. 29 northeast of Calistoga. Promoters created this name by combining California with the famed New York spa, Saratoga. While here you can visit fine restaurants like the Silverado, go for a balloon or glider ride, hit the mineral water spas, and ride the tramway up the mountain to the Moorish-style Sterling Vineyards Winery. Instead of rushing visitors through, Sterling offers self-guided tours and lawns and picnic tables where you can sample vintages in a leisurely manner. Open daily from 10:30 a.m. to 4:30 p.m. The tram costs $5. (707) 942-5151. Tasting at the Schramsberg Vineyard on Schramsberg Road (off S.R. 128 south of Calistoga) is by appointment only. The champagne cellars here are a state historic landmark. For permission to visit, call (707) 942-4558.

After visiting Schramsberg, drive south to the Silverado Museum at 1490 Library Lane in Saint Helena (open noon to 4:00 p.m. Tuesday through Sunday). It commemorates one of the winery's earliest boosters, Robert Louis Stevenson himself. In *Silverado Squatters*, he tells of sampling eighteen of founder Jacob Schram's vintages in a

single day! (The author's wine-tasting tour was a highlight of his honeymoon stay on Mount Saint Helena.)
This museum is near a downtown park that's perfect for lunch. Children will enjoy playing in the gazebo. History buffs may want to visit the Bale Grist Mill State Historic Park north of town off S.R. 29.

Numerous wineries such as Heitz, Robert Mondavi, and Martini beckon as you continue south on S.R. 29 toward Napa. For a more rustic experience, head down the east side of the valley on the Silverado Trail; it's the back road from Calistoga to Napa. The Napa Valley Wine Train will make an excellent addition to your visit. The 40-mile round-trip from Napa to St. Helena offers a pleasant overview of the region's vineyards and wineries. Lunch and dinner service is offered Tuesday through Sunday. The basic fare is $29. The lunch ride costs $45; the dinner trip is $57.50. The train departs from the depot at 1275 McKinstry Street in Napa at 11:30 a.m Tuesday through Friday and at 12:30 p.m. on weekends. The dinner train leaves at 6:30 p.m. Tuesday through Saturday. On Sunday the train leaves at 6:00 p.m. Call (707) 253-2111 or (800) 522-4142. For more information, contact the Napa Chamber of Commerce at 1900 Jefferson Street, P.O. Box 636, Napa 94558, (707) 226-7455, or the Calistoga Chamber of Commerce at 1458 Lincoln Avenue, Calistoga 94515, (707) 942-6333.

A good place to stay in this region is **La Residence**, a country inn at 4066 St. Helena Highway. (707) 253-0337. Rooms run $135 to $225. Ask for a room in the 18th-century Revival Mansion.

BERKELEY AND OAKLAND

ı our last day in California gives you a look at some of the finest views, museums, gardens, bookstores, restaurants, and parks in the state. You'll enjoy a memorable view of the Bay Area from the Berkeley campus, lunch at a temple of California cuisine, visit the state's best museum of Californiana, and take a charming tour of Oakland's Lake Merritt aboard a small paddlewheeler. This is a day that rounds out your trip with a chance to visit one of the nation's finest used bookstores and stop at an ice cream parlor you won't soon forget.

Suggested Schedule	
7:30 a.m.	Breakfast at your hotel.
8:15 a.m.	Drive to Berkeley.
9:30 a.m.	Visit the UC Berkeley Botanical Gardens.
10:30 a.m.	Tour the UC Campus area.
1:00 p.m.	Lunch at Chez Panisse.
3:00 p.m.	Oakland Museum.
5:30 p.m.	Dinner.
7:30 p.m.	Ice cream at Fenton's.

Travel Route: Sonoma to Berkeley and Oakland (50 miles)

Take S.R. 12 south to S.R. 37. Follow it to Interstate 80 west. Take the University Avenue/Berkeley exit east to Oxford Avenue. Turn left here to Hearst Street. Turn right to Gayley Road. Turn left on Rim Way and proceed around the football stadium to Centennial Drive. Continue east up the hill until you see the sign for the UC Botanical Gardens.

Berkeley/Oakland

Today you visit California's oldest university community and Jack London's hometown, Oakland. Together these cities offer some of the Bay Area's most important cultural resources. Stretching from the Bay flatlands up into the

East Bay hills, these towns are multi-ethnic, multi-cultural, and never dull. From the People's Republic of Berkeley— the only town in the United States with a sister city in El Salvador—to Oakland's booming Chinatown, the East Bay reflects California's coming emergence as a minority-dominated state. As you sample life here today, you'll see landmark buildings by architect Julia Morgan and Bernard Maybeck, visit what is arguably California's most famous restaurant, and enjoy a botanical treasure that most San Francisco visitors unfortunately miss.

Sightseeing Highlights

▲▲▲The University of California Botanical Gardens— More than 8,000 plants are found in this 30-acre Strawberry Canyon glen laced with streams and graced with Japanese gardens. Even the Japanese—no slouches when it comes to horticulture—flock here to see the vast outdoor collection of native Californian, African, South American, Australasian, and East Asian plants. There are major collections of rhododendrons, orchids, herbs, and insectivorous plants. Don't miss the greenhouses. The view looking down across Berkeley and San Francisco Bay is one you won't soon forget. If you're on a flexible schedule, continue on up Centennial Drive to the Lawrence Hall of Science. The hands-on exhibits here will entertain the whole family and the view is panoramic. Open seven days a week from 9:00 a.m. to 4:45 p.m. except Christmas. (510) 642-3343.

▲▲UC Campus—Head down Centennial Drive to Rim Way. Turn left and the street will become Prospect. Follow it to Channing, where you turn right past Telegraph Avenue to the Sather Gate Garage. Walk back up to Telegraph and turn right to the 178-acre UC Berkeley campus. The big building on your left as you enter Sproul Plaza (site of the famous Free Speech Movement battle of 1964) is Sproul Hall. Maps and brochures for self-guided tours and informational exhibits are available here at the visitor center, open 8:00 a.m. to noon and 1:00 to 5:00 p.m. Monday through Friday. Student-led tours are also offered Monday through Friday at 1:00 p.m. For information, call (510) 642-5215

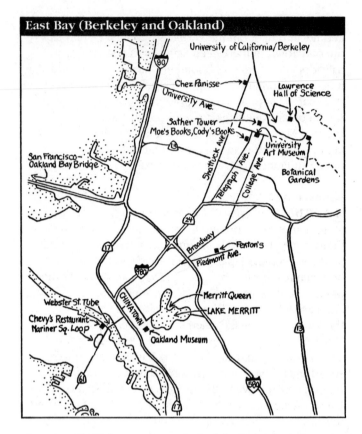

East Bay (Berkeley and Oakland)

▲Bancroft Library—The entrance to this outstanding research library is directly across from the Campanile Tower. Changing exhibits range from a first folio of Shakespeare to rare photographs of the great San Francisco earthquake and fire. Scholars come from all over the world to study the library's early Californiana, Mexicana, and literary manuscripts. Gallery hours are 9:00 a.m. to 5:00 p.m. Monday through Friday, and 1:00 to 5:00 p.m. Saturday. (510) 642-3781.

▲Campanile—At 50 cents, this ride to the Carillon Tower is a very good value. The elevator runs every three to five minutes from 10:00 a.m. to 4:15 p.m. You'll be rewarded with an excellent view of the campus.

▲Hearst Museum of Anthropology—This museum in

Kroeber Hall on Bancroft Way is dedicated to man's past. Exhibits range from prehistoric artifacts to art productions collected from Pacific Islanders in the 1960s. There are good exhibits on California Native Americans, including Ishi, the subject of Theodora Kroeber's classic *Ishi in Two Worlds*. The exhibit hall is open 10:00 a.m. to 4:00 p.m. Tuesday through Friday and noon to 4:30 p.m. weekends. Call (510) 642-3681.

▲▲**University Art Museum** at 2626 Bancroft Way displays Western and Oriental Art. The fan-shaped building leads visitors through spacious galleries via a network of spiral ramps Open 11:00 a.m. to 5:00 p.m. Wednesday through Sunday. (510) 642-0808.

▲**Moe's Books** at 2476 Telegraph Avenue, three blocks south of campus, is a used bookstore that amazes bibliophiles from far and near. Four neat, clean, well-organized floors offer a remarkable selection of quality titles. The prices are reasonable, and the books, by and large, are in excellent condition. (510) 849-2087. Next door is Cody's, Berkeley's largest bookstore for new titles. (510) 845-7852.

▲**Chez Panisse**, 1517 Shattuck Avenue, is reached by heading west on Channing Way to Shattuck. Turn right and continue north for about a mile. When Alice Waters opened her doors in 1972, she thought she was starting a restaurant. It quickly became an institution, and you now have to wait a month or more to get a reservation for the fixed-price dinners downstairs. Fortunately, she opened a café upstairs where you can sample her down-home California cooking with an accent on fresh, naturally grown ingredients. Waters has probably done more for roquette than any chef in the state, and you'll find the locally grown leaves and baby red lettuce in her garden salad. Endive, zen potatoes, rare eggplants, and exotic fruit like blood oranges frequently show up on the menu, as do Pacific oysters. Entrées include calzone, pizza, pasta, salmon, scallops in tarragon butter, and New York steak. Be sure to try the cakes and sherbets. Open Monday through Saturday 11:30 a.m. to 11:30 p.m. (510) 548-5525.

▲**Elmwood Pharmacy Fountain**, 2900 College Avenue, is a homey alternative with good soups, sandwiches, and

desserts. Come at the right moment and one of the 2 to 22
Days authors, Derk Richardson, or his wife, Robin (the
co-owner of the fountain), may take your order. This time
warp is reached by heading east on Channing Way to
College Avenue, turning right and continuing to Russell
Street, where you turn right again and park in the lot
directly behind the pharmacy. Yes, the milk shakes are
blended in frosty steel containers. (510) 843-1300.

▲▲▲Oakland Museum—Take Grand Avenue to
Harrison Street, then turn left to Lakeside Drive, which
becomes Madison; follow it to 11th Street and turn left to
1000 Oak Street and the Oakland Museum. Park in the
garage beneath the museum building. The museum is
also a short walk from the Lake Merritt BART station.
The perfect coda to your 22-day tour, this museum
embraces the length and breadth of your trip in galleries
devoted to the natural, political, artistic, and cultural heritage of California. Built on three levels with hanging gardens, lily ponds, and a lovely sculpture garden, this is the
place to answer some of the questions that may have been
raised by your journey. The environmental exhibits will
help you identify birds and wildlife you've seen along the
way. Design galleries take you from Mexican times
through the Victorian era and through art deco to the present day. Special exhibits cover everything from the story
of the Big Four railroad barons (Stanford, Huntington,
Harriman, and Crocker) to William Wrigley's Catalina road-
ster. From General Fremont to Richard M. Nixon, you'll
learn about the people who turned this modest pre-gold
rush land of 14,000 into a state of 28 million. The photographic exhibits are outstanding, and the gift shop has an
excellent selection of Californiana. There's a pleasant
restaurant and snack bar here. Open Wednesday through
Saturday 10:00 a.m. to 5:00 p.m., Sunday noon to 7:00
p.m. (510) 834-2413.

Food

If it's a warm night, consider **Chevy's**, a good, moderately
priced Mexican restaurant just ten minutes from downtown Oakland on the Alameda Estuary. Take a table out-

side and enjoy the sailboats cruising by on the waterfront. It's at 2400 Mariner Square Drive, Alameda. (510) 521-3768. Head north on 14th Street from the Oakland Museum and turn left on Webster to the Alameda Tube. Take the Mariner Square Drive exit, your first right after coming through the Tube to Mariner Square Loop. Follow this street to Mariner Square Drive and turn left to the restaurant. **Nan Yang** at 6048 College Avenue in Oakland is an excellent Burmese restaurant. (510) 655-3298. For excellent Vietnamese food, head to **Le Cheval** at 1007 Clay Street.. (510) 763-8495. **Bay Wolf**, 3853 Piedmont Avenue, Oakland, has an inviting deck and charming dining room where you can enjoy some of the East Bay's better French cooking. A worthy alternate to the often sold out Chez Panisse dining room in Berkeley. (510) 655-6004. Also worth a visit is **Ginger Island** at 1820 Fourth Street in Berkeley, (510) 644-0444, specializing in Asian-style cuisine—fresh ingredients. It's close to **Ratto's**, a fascinating international market that also serves lunch in a historic setting. Anyone with a bent for cooking will want to visit this venerable establishment at 821 Washington. (510) 832-6503. Oakland visitors may also want to try the fine pork ribs at **Flints**, 6609 Shattuck Avenue (near Alcatraz). (510) 653-0593. Wherever you dine, leave room for dessert.

All good things must come to an end. Why not have your grand finale at the ultimate ice cream parlor, known for its vast portions? That's **Fenton's Creamery**, 4226 Piedmont Avenue. From downtown Oakland take Broadway east to Piedmont Avenue and turn right. The jersey, black-and-tan, and hot fudge sundaes here will take your breath away; the banana splits could feed a family of four. This is the only ice cream parlor I know of where standard sundaes are officially classified as small. An East Bay landmark for decades, it's been imitated but never topped. No one has ever left this creamery hungry. (510) 658-7000.

Have a great trip home!

Other Books from John Muir Publications

Travel Books by Rick Steves
Asia Through the Back Door,
4th ed., 400 pp. $16.95
Europe 101: History, Art, and
Culture for the Traveler,
4th ed., 372 pp. $15.95
Mona Winks: Self-Guided
Tours of Europe's Top
Museums, 2nd ed., 456 pp.
$16.95
Rick Steves' Best of the
Baltics and Russia, 1995
ed. 144 pp. $9.95
Rick Steves' Best of Europe,
1995 ed., 544 pp. $16.95
Rick Steves' Best of France,
Belgium, and the
Netherlands, 1995 ed., 240
pp. $12.95
Rick Steves' Best of
Germany, Austria, and
Switzerland, 1995 ed., 240
pp. $12.95
Rick Steves' Best of Great
Britain, 1995 ed., 192 pp.
$11.95
Rick Steves' Best of Italy,
1995 ed., 208 pp. $11.95
Rick Steves' Best of
Scandinavia, 1995 ed., 192
pp. $11.95
Rick Steves' Best of Spain
and Portugal, 1995 ed., 192
pp. $11.95
Rick Steves' Europe Through
the Back Door, 13th ed.,
480 pp. $17.95
Rick Steves' French Phrase
Book, 2nd ed., 112 pp. $4.95
Rick Steves' German Phrase
Book, 2nd ed., 112 pp. $4.95
Rick Steves' Italian Phrase
Book, 2nd ed., 112 pp. $4.95
Rick Steves' Spanish and
Portuguese Phrase Book,
2nd ed., 288 pp. $5.95
Rick Steves'
French/German/Italian
Phrase Book, 288 pp. $6.95

A Natural Destination Series
Belize: A Natural Destination,
2nd ed., 304 pp. $16.95

Costa Rica: A Natural
Destination, 3rd ed., 400
pp. $17.95
Guatemala: A Natural
Destination, 336 pp. $16.95

Undiscovered Islands Series
Undiscovered Islands of the
Caribbean, 3rd ed., 264 pp.
$14.95
Undiscovered Islands of the
Mediterranean, 2nd ed., 256
pp. $13.95
Undiscovered Islands of the
U.S. and Canadian West
Coast, 288 pp. $12.95

For Birding Enthusiasts
The Birder's Guide to Bed
and Breakfasts: U.S.
and Canada, 288 pp.
$15.95
The Visitor's Guide to the
Birds of the Central
National Parks: U.S. and
Canada, 400 pp. $15.95
The Visitor's Guide to the
Birds of the Eastern
National Parks: U.S. and
Canada, 400 pp. $15.95
The Visitor's Guide to the
Birds of the Rocky
Mountain National Parks:
U.S. and Canada, 432 pp.
$15.95

Unique Travel Series
Each is 112 pages and $10.95
paperback.
Unique Arizona
Unique California
Unique Colorado
Unique Florida
Unique New England
Unique New Mexico
Unique Texas
Unique Washington

*2 to 22 Days Itinerary
Planners*
2 to 22 Days in the American
Southwest, 1995 ed., 192
pp. $11.95

2 to 22 Days in Asia, 192 pp. $10.95

2 to 22 Days in Australia, 192 pp. $10.95

2 to 22 Days in California, 1995 ed., 192 pp. $11.95

2 to 22 Days in Eastern Canada, 1995 ed., 240 pp. $12.95

2 to 22 Days in Florida, 1995 ed., 192 pp. $11.95

2 to 22 Days Around the Great Lakes, 1995 ed., 192 pp. $11.95

2 to 22 Days in Hawaii, 1995 ed., 192 pp. $11.95

2 to 22 Days in New England, 1995 ed., 192 pp. $11.95

2 to 22 Days in New Zealand, 192 pp. $10.95

2 to 22 Days in the Pacific Northwest, 1995 ed., 192 pp. $11.95

2 to 22 Days in the Rockies, 1995 ed., 192 pp. $11.95

2 to 22 Days in Texas, 1995 ed., 192 pp. $11.95

2 to 22 Days in Thailand, 192 pp. $10.95

22 Days Around the World, 264 pp. $13.95

Other Terrific Travel Titles

The 100 Best Small Art Towns in America, 224 pp. $12.95

Elderhostels: The Students' Choice, 2nd ed., 304 pp. $15.95

Environmental Vacations: Volunteer Projects to Save the Planet, 2nd ed., 248 pp. $16.95

A Foreign Visitor's Guide to America, 224 pp. $12.95

Great Cities of Eastern Europe, 256 pp. $16.95

Indian America: A Traveler's Companion, 3rd ed., 432 pp. $18.95

Interior Furnishings Southwest, 256 pp. $19.95

Opera! The Guide to Western Europe's Great Houses, 296 pp. $18.95

Paintbrushes and Pistols:

How the Taos Artists Sold the West, 288 pp. $17.95

The People's Guide to Mexico, 9th ed., 608 pp. $18.95

Ranch Vacations: The Complete Guide to Guest and Resort, Fly-Fishing, and Cross-Country Skiing Ranches, 3rd ed., 512 pp. $19.95

The Shopper's Guide to Art and Crafts in the Hawaiian Islands, 272 pp. $13.95

The Shopper's Guide to Mexico, 224 pp. $9.95

Understanding Europeans, 272 pp. $14.95

A Viewer's Guide to Art: A Glossary of Gods, People, and Creatures, 144 pp. $10.95

Watch It Made in the U.S.A.: A Visitor's Guide to the Companies that Make Your Favorite Products, 272 pp. $16.95

Parenting Titles

Being a Father: Family, Work, and Self, 176 pp. $12.95

Preconception: A Woman's Guide to Preparing for Pregnancy and Parenthood, 232 pp. $14.95

Schooling at Home: Parents, Kids, and Learning, 264 pp., $14.95

Teens: A Fresh Look, 240 pp. $14.95

Automotive Titles

The Greaseless Guide to Car Care Confidence, 224 pp. $14.95

How to Keep Your Datsun/Nissan Alive, 544 pp. $21.95

How to Keep Your Subaru Alive, 480 pp. $21.95

How to Keep Your Toyota Pickup Alive, 392 pp. $21.95

How to Keep Your VW Alive, 25th Anniversary ed., 464 pp. spiral bound $25

TITLES FOR YOUNG READERS AGES 8 AND UP

American Origins Series
Each is 48 pages and $12.95 hardcover.
Tracing Our English Roots
Tracing Our German Roots
Tracing Our Irish Roots
Tracing Our Italian Roots
Tracing Our Japanese Roots
Tracing Our Jewish Roots
Tracing Our Polish Roots

Bizarre & Beautiful Series
Each is 48 pages, $9.95 paperback, and $14.95 hardcover.
Bizarre & Beautiful Ears
Bizarre & Beautiful Eyes
Bizarre & Beautiful Feelers
Bizarre & Beautiful Noses
Bizarre & Beautiful Tongues

Environmental Titles
Habitats: Where the Wild Things Live, 48 pp. $9.95
The Indian Way: Learning to Communicate with Mother Earth, 114 pp. $9.95
Rads, Ergs, and Cheeseburgers: The Kids' Guide to Energy and the Environment, 108 pp. $13.95
The Kids' Environment Book: What's Awry and Why, 192 pp. $13.95

Extremely Weird Series
Each is 48 pages, $9.95 paperback, and $14.95 hardcover.
Extremely Weird Bats
Extremely Weird Birds
Extremely Weird Endangered Species
Extremely Weird Fishes
Extremely Weird Frogs
Extremely Weird Insects
Extremely Weird Mammals
Extremely Weird Micro Monsters
Extremely Weird Primates
Extremely Weird Reptiles
Extremely Weird Sea Creatures
Extremely Weird Snakes
Extremely Weird Spiders

Kidding Around Travel Series
All are 64 pages and $9.95 paperback, except for *Kidding Around Spain* and *Kidding Around the National Parks of the Southwest*, which are 108 pages and $12.95 paperback.
Kidding Around Atlanta
Kidding Around Boston, 2nd ed.
Kidding Around Chicago, 2nd ed.
Kidding Around the Hawaiian Islands
Kidding Around London
Kidding Around Los Angeles
Kidding Around the National Parks of the Southwest
Kidding Around New York City, 2nd ed.
Kidding Around Paris
Kidding Around Philadelphia
Kidding Around San Diego
Kidding Around San Francisco
Kidding Around Santa Fe
Kidding Around Seattle
Kidding Around Spain
Kidding Around Washington, D.C., 2nd ed.

Kids Explore Series
Written by kids for kids, all are $9.95 paperback.
Kids Explore America's African American Heritage, 128 pp.
Kids Explore the Gifts of Children with Special Needs, 128 pp.
Kids Explore America's Hispanic Heritage, 112 pp.
Kids Explore America's Japanese American Heritage, 144 pp.

Masters of Motion Series
Each is 48 pages and $9.95 paperback.
How to Drive an Indy Race Car
How to Fly a 747
How to Fly the Space Shuttle

Rainbow Warrior Artists Series
Each is 48 pages, $14.95 hardcover, and $9.95 paperback.
Native Artists of Africa
Native Artists of Europe
Native Artists of North America

Rough and Ready Series
Each is 48 pages, $12.95 hardcover, and $9.95 paperback.
Rough and Ready Cowboys
Rough and Ready Homesteaders
Rough and Ready Loggers
Rough and Ready Outlaws and Lawmen
Rough and Ready Prospectors
Rough and Ready Railroaders

X-ray Vision Series
Each is 48 pages and $9.95 paperback.
Looking Inside the Brain
Looking Inside Cartoon Animation
Looking Inside Caves and Caverns
Looking Inside Sports Aerodynamics
Looking Inside Sunken Treasures
Looking Inside Telescopes and the Night Sky

Ordering Information
Please check your local bookstore for our books, or call **1-800-888-7504** to order direct. All orders are shipped via UPS; see chart below to calculate your shipping charge for U.S. destinations. **No post office boxes please; we must have a street address to ensure delivery.** If the book you request is not available, we will hold your check until we can ship it. Foreign orders will be shipped surface rate unless otherwise requested; please enclose $3 for the first item and $1 for each additional item.

For U.S. Orders

Totaling	Add
Up to $15.00	$4.25
$15.01 to $45.00	$5.25
$45.01 to $75.00	$6.25
$75.01 or more	$7.25

Methods of Payment
Check, money order, American Express, MasterCard, or Visa. We cannot be responsible for cash sent through the mail. For credit card orders, include your card number, expiration date, and your signature, or call **1-800-888-7504**. American Express card orders can only be shipped to billing address of cardholder. Sorry, no C.O.D.'s. Residents of sunny New Mexico, add 6.25% tax to total.

Address all orders and inquiries to:
> John Muir Publications
> P.O. Box 613
> Santa Fe, NM 87504
> (505) 982-4078
> (800) 888-7504